Jaso

Helmet

The story of how a soldier's helmet found 65 years ago brought families from two nations together.

Linda Barron Heinrich
with
Brian Heinrich

Woodmoor Publishing
Hagerstown, Maryland

ISBN: 978-0-9825389-0-6
Cover Design: Brian Heinrich and Alex Harrison

Photographs provided by: Jacques Cabannes, Edward J.
Nayes, Rene Brideau, Frederic Blais, Stephane Bignon,
Brian Heinrich, Army Archives, and Families of Soldiers.

Printed in United States of America

To order additional copies of Jason's Helmet contact:
Woodmoor Publishing Co.
17601 Forest Glen Circle
Hagerstown, Maryland 21740
                or
Email: info@jasonshelmet.com

Website: www.jasonshelmet.com

ii

To Monica

Dedicated to:

Roger Pillu,
Arthur LeNoble (in memory),
Roger Bignon and Genevieve Bignon,
René and Marie Antoinette Brideau,
Frederic and Houda Blais,
Mayor Marcel Gautier
Mayor Jean-Marc Allain
and the
people of Normandy, France

Linda Barton Heinrich

*Although this book is about only six soldiers
who sacrificed their lives for freedom,
my hope is that all soldiers will be honored
by the commitment I feel in sharing this story.
As Dad stated, "One is not more important
than the rest."*

Linda Barron Heinrich

Table of Contents

Part I

Part II

Prologue

The events recorded in this story have culminated into the most enriching experience of my life. Through my research I have been touched by the five families of the soldiers who died with my uncle, Jason H. Barron, during World War II. We shared a common bond that was brought to life by people 3,000 miles away in a foreign land.

It was the determination of the people of Louge-sur-Maire, France, to find the family of Jason H. Barron and return the helmet left behind after his death. They continued to honor the memories of the six young men who sacrificed their lives for the liberation of their village. Now, after sixty-five years, they wanted the families of these men to know they were not forgotten.

This is the story of how the journey of a helmet found in 1944 brought families from two nations together and gave them peace.

Part I

"as these bells ring,
the honored dead rest,
and liberty lives"

Brittany Cemetery Bell Tower

1

The Testimony

Finally the airplane reaches the required altitude and levels. After driving three hours to the airport, hustling through security, waiting two hours to be called to the gate, and trying to ward off preflight jitters, now I can relax.

The tone sounds as the seatbelt sign changes to show we can unbuckle. I know to keep mine buckled in the event of turbulence. The flight attendants are preparing to serve our dinner. It's going to be a long trip, but it will be worth it.

Dad seems to be settled in for the flight. Usually he fights my husband for the window seat. However, Dad decides to take the aisle seat because he likes to get up and stretch frequently on long trips. If anyone knew how much trouble I had getting my father to come on this trip, I would surely get an award for persistence. My nephew, Ryan, his wife Holly and their four-year-old son are also settled.

Reaching down into my carry-on for a magazine, I notice the binder. It has been growing for two and a half years, ever since they found Jason's family – my family. Without hesitation, I pull it out and open to page one. There is the picture of the helmet, the reason for this journey.

"We have the helmet of your brother."

Two and a half years earlier, the letter arrived. In imperfectly-translated French it read, "We are seeking the family of First Lieutenant Jason H. Barron who was killed in action in France during World War II. The helmet of this young soldier was found sixty-five years ago. We wish to return it to his family."

My father handed me the letter and shook his head, "It's a scam. I read a story in the newspaper a couple of months ago about people contacting families of soldiers and selling them fake relics."

I replied, "But Dad, they aren't asking for money."

"They will. It's a scam," he repeated.

Dad was a product of the times. Every day it seemed we heard about someone being fooled out of their savings for retirement or their identity being stolen. Dad was wise to be so careful.

"There's an email address here. Let me see what I can find out." I, however, was just as sure that this was authentic as my father was sure it was a scam. Besides, I wanted it to be true.

I sent a message to the email address on the letter. René Brideau replied, "We have the helmet of your uncle …."

Over the next two years, René kept us updated on what was being planned, but they were scarce on the details. They wanted the family of Jason H. Barron to come to France to receive the helmet, and that's all we knew. Dad had a problem with this.

"Why can't they just mail it to us?" he questioned.

On this trip, Dad would come to understand why it was so important that we go to France. René Brideau was a friend of Roger Bignon. Roger had served in the Algerian War with René 's father-in-law. René was asked to find the family of Jason H. Barron so that the helmet could be returned.

By searching the Army Archives, René located the name of a sister, Anthea Barron Hankey of Hagerstown, Maryland. She had written a letter to The Adjunct General requesting information about the circumstances of her brother's death. René had a copy of the letter that she had written. However, the year that she wrote it was 1958. It had been fourteen years since Jason had died in 1944, and still, all the family knew was that he had been killed in action somewhere in France.

With that small piece of information on Anthea's letter to the Adjunct General, he began his search. He sent letters to her address. Sadly, Anthea and her husband, William, had died at a fairly early age during the 1960's. René, however, managed to find and contact Samuel Hankey, William's brother, through the internet.

Samuel was aware that Anthea's brother, Emerson S. Barron, had moved to Hagerstown from Somerset, Pennsylvania. He took the letters to Emerson.

On December 15, 2006, René received a very skeptical inquiry through a letter from Emerson S. Barron. René responded to Emerson, giving him the history of the finding of the helmet. He requested that the family come to France to reclaim the helmet. René explained that he already had experience locating the families of American soldiers. His father had rescued an American aviator and René later reunited the families of the aviator's crew.

The connection between the people of Lougé-sur-Maire and the helmet, which had been found after my uncle's body was removed, was unmistakable. With each email that René would send us, he would have a picture or a document attached, giving us evidence of their sincerity. As René spoke of my uncle, there was little doubt of the affection these people felt for this soldier who had given his life for their liberation. And, there was no doubt that they were determined to honor the family who mourned the loss of this soldier who made the ultimate sacrifice.

On August 17, 1944, two young men were on their way to a nearby town to gather information about the battle that had recently occurred when they happened upon a gruesome scene. Here is the testimony of one of them that René provided which helped solidify our decision in making this trip.

TESTIMONY OF MR. Roger PILLU
(Translated by Computer from French-Imperfect)

History of the helmet of an American soldier killed August 17,1944, the day of the liberation of the small city of LOUGE-SUR- MAIRE (Department of Orne).

It is about an anecdote told by a witness who evokes his memories of which [are] most prominent and also the saddest the macabre discovery of six American soldiers killed this August 17, 1944.

This noteworthy day I was 24 years old, I was then at the hamlet of "La Tirardière" where I lived the last days of the occupation at the scene of The Battle of Normandy, the famous pocket of Cliff, after the irresistible thrust of the American army followed the discomfiture [humiliation] of the German troops.

The night of this August 17 was decisive after the hard and last fights in the region of FROMENTEL, and at dawn it was a surprise and joy to see [what] happened by the first American soldiers, our liberators.

...In the afternoon, taking advantage of a lull of the cannonades, I decided with Arthur LENOBLE, my near neighbor, to go to "La Métrière", the neighboring hamlet to have news.

To midway, close to an abandoned German tank, our attention was attracted by a vast awning spread on ground blocking the passage [road].

Intrigued by this camouflage, we could not imagine that were below pell-mell [disorderly frantic rush] hidden six American soldiers. They lay killed probably in an ambush and were hidden under this awning by mates [during the] fight.

Horrified by this macabre discovery, we decided ... to [alert] the American reinforced division that camped not far from the borough.

We arrived without clutters [difficulty] to the camp and controlled [proceeded] toward the headquarters ... to announce the [events]. The Captain took us on board of his jeep to the place of the drama.

There, I remember some details, the Captain had himself raised the awning and [searched] his six dead mates. He had withdrawn the watch bracelet of one or two and had given of the orders to removed the spoils deadly [bodies] of his glorious soldiers quickly.

I was therefore the witness of this very sad and unforgettable spectacle who impressed me a lot.

The captain didn't remain anymore at the site. Left behind were the helmets of these heroes of which one carried the name of BARRON struck by a bullet. I collected it therefore and conserved in memories of these [events]. My sister, Denise DUMONS, will come to put some flowers … where First Lieutenant Jason BARRON and his five soldiers have been killed.

Since, six decades went by and it was on the occasion of the 60th birthday of the liberation of the small city of LOUGE-SUR-MAIRE that I had the happy idea to come in pilgrimage August 17, 2004 on the [same place] of his hero's sacrifice, and to [give] his helmet to my friend Roger BIGNON that lives in "La Métrière" close to the place of the drama.

Thanks to his fruitful research, knowing [Jason's] name and his [identification] number, they could [find] his tomb where he rests at the cemetery for U. S. soldiers, at Saint James (Department of la Manche), and he has just discovered now his family … in the United States.

It was unexpected after so [many] year, and to crown all research with success, he remains to hand to his family's member that will come in France, this famous helmet [real relic] that comes back to him one day only.

We didn't forget what we owe to our American and British allies, and to their thousands of dead for the liberty. The debt of France towards them is imprescriptible.

The translation of the messages from France was often a challenge to read, but with a little effort it was easier to understand. Roger Pillu had honored these soldiers who gave the ultimate sacrifice for his liberation. He took it personally and acted on it by reporting his discovery to the nearest encampment. His sister placed flowers on the site of their death.

When he says, "he remains to hand to his family's member that will come in France this famous helmet real relic," I believe he is saying that he is happy that he lived long enough to be able to return the helmet with gratitude himself. "We didn't forget....." was contrary to distorted rumors we've heard over the years that the French people did not care for Americans. This witness from Normandy of my uncle's sacrifice reminded me that the debt that was owed to these soldiers was "imprescriptible" or... impossible to remove, or to deny.

With information that dad provided, René was also able to contact my aunt, Virginia McAlister, who lives in Jacksonville, Florida. "Ginny" was fifteen when the older brother she so admired reported for duty after being home on leave.

So here we are. Two and a half years later, I am on an airplane with my family, hoping to give my dad closure to losing his brother in 1944, while at the same time making the dream of the people of a small French village come true. I am thrilled that Dad is with us. I am also thrilled that my nephew and his young family will experience this firsthand with us.

Roger Pillu, 24, is pictured here with his sister, Denise Dumons, and his nieces.

2
The Soldier from Somerset

First Lieutenant Jason H. Barron
Born 1920
Age at Death: 23
Somerset, Pennsylvania
KIA August 17, 1944
Lougé-sur-Maire

I turn to the next page in the binder. I see two pictures of a young man of twenty-three. In one picture he is in his military uniform; the other with maps under his arm in a battle zone. He is the uncle I never got a chance to meet. However, I felt as if I knew him through the stories my dad, aunts and uncles have told.

Lieutenant Jason H. BARRON
3rd Armored Division
36th Armored Infantry Regiment

I recall very clearly when I first learned that my dad had a brother who was killed in World War II. At the time I was six years old. We were watching television and someone had died on the show. I asked my dad, "Daddy, do you know anyone who died?"

Dad was silent. A dark, solemn look overtook my dad's face. "Yes, I had a brother and a sister who died."

"Why did they die, Daddy?"

"My brother, Jason was killed in a war and my sister, Bernice was sick."

Dad got up and walked down the steps to the basement. I went into my bedroom and I cried. I felt as if I had done a bad thing. I made my daddy sad. That night when my mother came in to kiss me good-night she told me that both daddy's brother and sister had died nine years earlier. She explained that dad was very close to them, especially his brother, and he still missed them very much.

Mother eased my guilt, but I never forgot that look of sadness on my dad's face. I would see it over and over again as the years passed. Any time Jason's name was mentioned, I saw it. Any time the war was mentioned, it appeared.

Recently dad told me of a recurring dream that he has been having since Jason's death. He talked about waking up crying many nights thinking of his brother.

"The nightmare comes. Jason arrives in a car. He walks up the sidewalk toward the house. Dad is waiting on the porch for him. Jason gets close. He looks up at Dad, but he doesn't speak. The dream ends."

I am my father's daughter. Tears come easily when I think of Jason. I suppose it is because his death caused so much pain to my father and my grandmother, grandfather, and the rest of my family. Aunt Virginia reacts the same way.

When I asked her to come along for this trip to France, she murmured, "I can't. It still hurts too much."

I have three sons. Brent is 32, Benjamin is 25 and Nicholas is 24 years old. It is amazing to think of the responsibility that Jason and other soldiers had at the same young age.

3

The Family

Now I turn to a picture of a large family - page three. The trees in the background, the suits and dresses, and the young man in the uniform tell me the picture was taken in the early summer of 1943. I wonder how someone can get nine children and two parents together for a picture when I can't get my three sons together for a family portrait without threatening them.

This was obviously taken in the days before the photographers said, "Say Cheese!" Only Aunt Virginia in the top left-hand corner has the slightest hint of a smile. Knowing what a fun-loving person she is, I can imagine that she must have amused herself with a happy thought on such a pretty Sunday afternoon.

I look at each face in the picture. I wonder if they have any idea of their destiny.

Starting in the back row on the left stands Virginia, the youngest daughter. She will be one of the two remaining family members to live into the twenty-

The Ira and Anna Belle Barron Family:
(Back row) Virginia, Anthea, Jason, Bernice, Clair,
(Front row) Ethan, Elbert, Papa, Mama, Wally, Emerson

first century. She has always had a wonderful attitude and a love for life. In 1995, she will visit Jason's grave at the Brittany American Cemetery in St. James, France, with her son, Steve, his wife, Nancy, and their two children. She will not be able to attend the ceremonies in France in 2009 for it will be far too emotional.

To Virginia's right in the picture is Anthea. She took responsibility for looking after her sisters and brothers. Anthea and her husband, Bill, will both work at Fairchild Industries building airplanes during the war. They will own a cabin along the Potomac River and the Chesapeake and Ohio Canal near Clear Spring, Maryland. She will swim across the Potomac River and back almost every day at

Four Locks during the summer. This will be the gathering place for many Barron picnics and weekend get-togethers. Many of my most joyful childhood memories will happen at this cabin.

Jason appears in his military uniform. He is the middle child - four older siblings and four younger. His bride will be widowed before the end of the war. The exact circumstances of death will elude the family until May 2009 when they will be invited to take a trip to a small town in France.

This will be Bernice's last picture. She will be remembered as a very kind-hearted person. On many occasions, she brings little gifts for her younger brothers and sisters. My older cousin, Audrey, recalls a memory when she was in the hospital. She always had candy for the visitors. Her daughter will be raised by her stepmother.

Clair, the youngest son, will grow up to serve in the Korean War. Being a very bright young man, he will be advanced to military intelligence. To earn money to pay for commercial flying school at Fort Lauderdale, Florida, he will give private flying lessons. He will teach me to ride a bicycle and I will tell him that I am going to marry him when I grow up. I will cry my heart out when on New Year's Eve in 1958 he loses his life at the age of 27, while giving a flying lesson. His plane will crash into the Atlantic Ocean, 500 yards from shore. At 3:15

in the afternoon, there will be many witnesses on the beach. The cause of the plane crash will be documented as mechanical failure.

Starting in the left of the front row are Ethan and Elbert who will become successful businessmen. Ethan, the oldest, will be an entrepreneur. He will be successful building several businesses - trucking, selling fertilizer and feed, and owning a large motel. Elbert will be a building contractor and County Plumbing Inspector. They will be known for their honesty and integrity.

Papa and Mama Barron are next. They share the responsibility for raising a fine family. They are farmers, and Papa owns a coal business in Hagerstown, Maryland. The family isn't rich, but according to Dad they never went hungry, even during the depression. Together, they will instill a strong moral and work ethic in their children.

Wally will serve in the war in the European Campaign. He will be present when the army finds the German death camps. He will have deep emotional trauma that would haunt him for the rest of his life. Later, this will come to be known as post-traumatic stress syndrome.

Last, but not least, is Emerson, my father. His teacher at a one room school house had held him back one year for getting into a fight on the last day of school in the second grade. The teacher said, "Do you want me to hold you back a year?"

Dad's smart-alec remark was, "Yeah!"

Her word was good. Dad repeated the second grade.

Later, he will give that teacher credit for saving his life because it will delay him entering the service for one year until near the end of the war. During his time in the Army Air Force he will experience many close calls including having to bail out in the Bermuda Triangle when his plane's instruments stop functioning. He will tread water for hours and be on the verge of giving up before the rescue ship finds him. He will come to be known as the 'Red Barron'. For forty years, this nickname will long endure as a successful business in Williamsport, Maryland.

4

The Beauty and the Maverick

Eunice Barron

I wish I had known the beautiful woman on page four of my binder. She was movie star beautiful. Her name was Eunice. Jason was stationed at Fort Smith, Arkansas. She was the ticket girl at the local theater. The first time Jason saw her, he said to his buddy, "I'm gonna marry that girl."

Jason would go to the movies just so he could buy a ticket and see the girl he planned to marry. For him, it was love at first sight. For her, it was different. She had heard he was a maverick. Finally, love won out and they were married on February 6, 1943. They would spend ten months together and eight months thousands of miles apart.

Jason and Eunice were married for 18 months

It took me a long time before I got the courage to read the next four pages in the binder - the letter. I had put it in the binder and started to read it many times. It seemed as though I was sneaking into their personal lives where I shouldn't be and I would stop. When I finally read the letter, I learned so much about this couple and the great love they shared.

Mar 23, 1944

My Darling Eunice,

    I received four real sweet letters from you last night. One of them must have come by way of China as it was posted February 15th. The other three were March 7, 8, and 9th.

    Where I am writing it is a bit chilly. So, I'll have to rush to keep warm. Every once in a while we come out in the field for a two or three day problem. This is one of those times.

    I'm glad you decided to stay in Oregon. I would much rather see you there, than back in Ft. Smith. Somehow or other I disapprove of you near an army camp. Maybe it's because I am jealous.

Then too I know how soldiers can wolf. That is, some of them.

Now I'll answer a question that usually comes up once a month. I am at the point where I expect one letter a month where you ask me if am true to you; and every time I answer that same question. No, honey I wouldn't even think of going out with another girl. Though you don't trust me Darling, far be it for me to go against my better judgment and do you that way. I love you too much for you to have any silly ideas or thoughts pertaining to me dating an English girl. I'll tell you what I'll do - If I go out with a girl - I'll write and tell you about it; I can tell you now that you will never receive such a letter because I never will go out. I would like you to know that it hurts me having you not trust me. I always trust you and never think for a minute that you would step out on me. However, I must admit that if you are I wouldn't believe it unless I saw it with my own eyes. Have you ever been asked for a date since you have been in Oregon? If so how many times? Honey -

Remember that I love only you and couldn't do anything to hurt you. You are a wonderful, sweet, beautiful, and very good wife - I never want to lose you, Honey. If you feel like asking me the same question next month - go right ahead and I'm sure you will receive the same answer as I have already stated.

We soon will have a little cash saved up. Thanks to you, Honey! You are real nice for taking care of our future; and that is what you and I must live for now. Let's just hope and pray that future isn't too far away. Yes! Honey we were divided by about six hundred miles of land last spring at this time, and I did not know when I would be in your arms again. It's a little different this spring. Now, all we can do is hope that next spring finds us different than the past two. Let's hope that we are together as near as any two people of the opposite sex can get. How about that?

I don't recall if I told you or not - But, don't send me any more cigarettes until I ask you again. Thanks for the package you have sent. I didn't receive it yet, but am patiently waiting. I hope it doesn't come while I am out here in the field. Sooner have it when I'm in camp, then I can take better care of it.

All the fellows from my platoon are grouped around me - and they want to write this letter for me - well I would let them, only they could never know what a wonderful person they are writing to unless they met you. So - I'll continue writing.

I had letters from both Anthea and Bernice. Anthea is getting along okay, but Bernice is pretty sick. She must really feel miserable. Honey, you take good care of yourself for me - I want to come to you just the way I left. And as for me I'll be back much sweeter & nicer. Too bad you didn't get back to see Elbert and Ruth when you were in Somerset. I haven't heard from them since I have been in England. They will probably give me heck about it. Be sure you see them this summer when you go there. They are really very nice people. I like Elbert as one of my best brothers.

26

Just like you preferring one of your
sisters to another that is the way with me.
I guess you and I are a little too partial.
Heck.

Well, honey this about winds up what
I have to say this morning. Remember
though that I am yours completely. I
love you every minute of the day and
am anxiously waiting for that day of
days when we can share our love and
feelings arm in arm rather than across
the great big sea. Honey, I love you
forever.

Always and Forever,
Your Jay

P.S. I Love You Mostest
P.S. Jr. I just about froze writing this. I
hope you appreciate it and excuse all
mistakes.

I Love you, Honey

Eunice had married a good-looking guy. She had to ask the questions that were reinforced all around her. Were you still true? Do you still love me? Jason had to answer those questions. He answered directly, closing his letter with, "Honey, I love you forever," and post scripted with a young and playful response, "I love you the mostest."

Jason was concerned about Eunice being on her own. He wanted her to go and stay with his parents for awhile. She arrived in Somerset in her red convertible in early August as Jason requested.

5

Summer of Sorrow

The summer of 1944 would hold double sorrows for the Barron family. Bernice, the beloved sister, would die in July of an illness that was never diagnosed. Little Martha Ann, the apple of her mother's eye, was three years old and without a mother. Her father would go on to remarry and Martha Ann would be treated harshly.

Two more sons would break their mother's heart as they too become soldiers in the United States Army. Dad, like most veterans, never spoke about his time in World War II. Two years ago he received a letter from one of his B-29 crew members. The man's granddaughter was writing a book and he asked Dad to send some of his memories of their B-29 days. I would be privy to stories of experiences that he kept to himself all these years. He gave me handwritten copies of his stories and asked me to type them. I will forever cherish these stories. I had never realized how much he respected the men in his crew and how close he had come to dying.

Like thousands of boys in the 1940's, Jason had stepped up to the call of his country and enlisted. He graduated from Officer's Candidate School in Fort Benning, Georgia, as a Second Lieutenant. Later he became a First Lieutenant. In the spring of 1944, he was home on leave. A call came during the night and he was instructed to report to the base. The brothers and sisters crawled out of bed and lined-up in the dimly lit kitchen at three o'clock in the morning. Each one hugged him and said goodbye. After he went out the door, his mother turned and said, "We will never see him again.

On August 17, 1944, a young French farm boy named Roger Bignon stands at the kitchen window. There is a bright flash of light and the a loud sound of an explosion. Six young soldiers lie dead 330 yards from his house.

The dreaded telegram bearing the news arrived a few days later.

Eunice was staying with the Barron Family at that time. Virginia was 15 years old. She told me that Eunice slept beside her in her bed for many nights after the telegram arrived. She said Eunice cried so hard that the pillows were drenched.

Aunt Virginia sadly told me, "Papa Barron cried too."

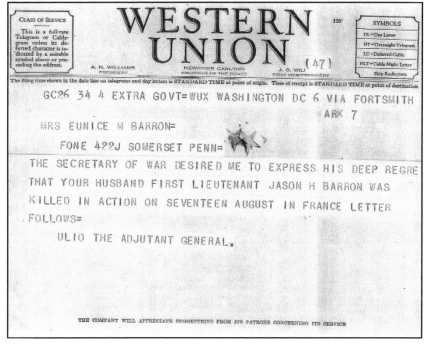

Telegram from the war department

The words from Jason's last letter to Eunice are haunting.

"Now all we can do is hope that next spring will be different from the last two."

There would never be another spring for Jason.

My Dad was in basic training at Buckingham Field in Biloxi, Mississippi, when he received word that his sister had died. Although he was expecting the bad news, it was a blow. A few weeks later, the only letter his father had ever written to him arrived. Unfortunately it would contain information that would shock him to the core and deprive him of his brother forever.

Aunt Virginia told me that Eunice requested that the small death benefit of twenty dollars per month be sent to Grandmother Barron. Eunice said that she was young and would be able to get a job. Eunice knew that times were tough and her mother-in-law needed the money for the younger children. Virginia said that every time the check came, her mother would cry.

On American Red Cross stationery a friend of Jason's wrote this letter to find out information three years after his death:

Adjutant General's Office
Officers' Section
 Washington, D.C.

I would like to get some information regarding a friend of mine from a former outfit. I heard he was killed in action. Jason Barron was a Lieutenant in the 62nd Armed Infantry Regiment, 14th Armed Division in 1943. If he has been listed KIA or MIA,

I would like to have the last known address of his wife. Last I heard she was located in Fort Smith, Ark. They were married either the latter part of January or first part of February.

George D. Covey
San Francisco, California

I realized when reading this, it was written three days before I was born.

Here is the reply:

AGPO-CG 201 Barron, Jason H.
(15 August 47) 01296652

2 September 1947
Mr. George D. Covey
San Francisco 22, California

Dear Mr. Covey:

In reply to your letter on 15 August 1947 requesting information concerning First Lieutenant Jason H. Barron, I regret to advise you that he was killed in action in France on 17 August 1944.

Lieutenant Barron's wife may be addressed as Mrs. Eunice M. Barron, 1821 North 3rd Street, Fort Smith, Arkansas.

I trust this information will be of assistance to you and wish to assure you of the gratitude of a grateful nation of your accomplishments in the past conflict.

Sincerely yours,

Edward F. Witsell,
Major General
The Adjunct General of the Army

It contained the official seal from Family Relations, Room 5C826, The Pentagon, 29, Aug. 47.

I learned that George Covey had served in the 62nd Armed Infantry Regiment, 14th Armed Division with Uncle Jason before he was sent to France. They may have been separated on the battlefield with different assignments, but still they had shared similar hardships and developed the unique type of friendship that only soldiers have. George had a bond with Jason deep enough to inquire about his status three years later. He cared enough to want to express his regrets to his friend's widow.

These were confusing times. The whereabouts of hundreds, perhaps thousands, of soldiers was unknown. Now the war was over and I imagine that when George came home, he thought about the friends he made during the war. He heard that Jason may have been missing in action or have been killed. This prompted the letter.

Soldiers develop a very true friendship in times of war. The bond of trust is never forgotten. For instance, my father stayed in contact with members of his B-29 crew as long as they lived.

Most have died. He is still very close to Bob Forgeng, the radio operator on his plane. For decades, the crew of the B-29 visited at each other's homes for the annual reunion. We never missed one of these reunions. Just like my father and Bob Forgeng, had Jason survived, I am sure that he and George would have been lifelong friends.

6
Deeds Not Words

Silver Star
For gallantry in action against an opposing armed force.

Seventeen days before his death, Jason earned the Silver Star Medal for Heroism. Jason was proving himself on the battlefield. He belonged to a division whose motto was, "Deeds, not Words." He must have exemplified this motto because he had earned the respect of his men and his superior officers. The Silver Star is the third highest medal that can be earned by a soldier. As a First Lieutenant, he had displayed courage and leadership when he led a counteroffensive against an enemy attack. This action was commended by Brigadier General Rose who commanded the award be given.

First Name			Middle Initial		Serial No.		Grade
BARRON	JASON		K	H	01295652		1st Lt.
ganization					Foreign		Others
36th Armd Inf. Regt.							
dquarters			Station or APO		G.O. No.	Section	Date
3d Armd Div.			253		35	II	17 Aug
e of Award					Posthumous		DO NOT WI COLUMN E
Silver Star Medal					No		
-Leaf Clusters				Number	Posthumous		
Command of					Amended	Revoked	
Brig. Gen. Rose							

CITATION

For gallantry in action in ***. on 31 July 1944. When Lieutenant Barron's platoon received the brunt of a vicious enemy counter-attack he succeeded in locating a mortar squad to lend support to his platoon. He also borrowed a .50 cal. machine gun from friendly troops and directed the fire of the mortar and the machine gun on the advancing enemy. His action immediately stopped the counter-attack and forced the enemy to withdraw to the positions they had previously held. The superior leadership and personal bravery displayed by Lieutenant Barron was an inspiration to his men and reflects great credit upon himself and the Armed Forces.

Entered military service from Pennsylvania

Jason's Silver Star Citation issued August 17, 1944.

The citation read:

"For gallantry in action on 31 July 1944. When Lieutenant Barron's platoon received the brunt of a vicious enemy counter-attack he succeeded in locating a mortar squad to lend support to his platoon. He also borrowed a .50 caliber machine gun from friendly troops and directed the fire of the mortar and the machine gun on the advancing enemy. His action immediately stopped the counter-attack and forced the enemy to withdraw to the positions they had previously held. The superior leadership and personal bravery displayed by Lieutenant Barron was an inspiration to his men and reflects great credit upon himself and the Armed Forces."

Division motto - DEEDS NOT WORDS

To our regret, Jason would not have known that he received the Silver Star Medal. General Rose issued the citation on August 17, 1944, the day that Jason was KIA.

My father was very proud of his brother.

7
"Purple Heart Corner"

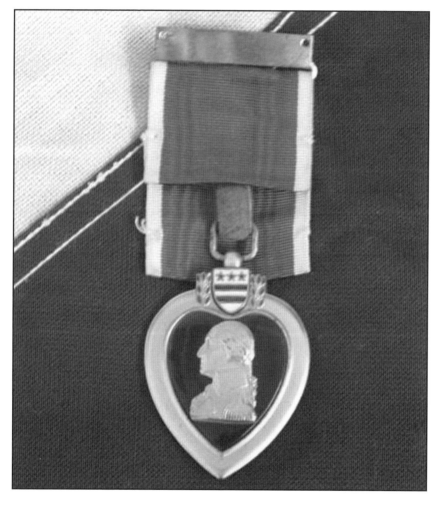

Oldest award that is still given to members of the U.S. military for being wounded or killed.

René sent me an official-looking map that must have come from the military archives. It is heavy with detail and very difficult to read. What seems clear is the objective of the Third Armored Division to divide into a three-pronged attack to surround the little town of Fromentel just north of them. I included a simplified Google map to show Uncle Jason's path with his platoon, as indicated by the solid line.

Later, I would learn that the area near Fromentel would come to be known as "Purple Heart Corner" because of the heavy losses sustained by the United States troops.

René had sent a military report of the 3rd Armored Division plan to take Fromentel, France. Unfortunately, this report began on August 17, the day Uncle Jason and his men were killed. My husband and I wanted to know more about the days leading up to that day. We searched the internet for more information and found a site specifically written about the 'Spearhead'.

It is easier to let the experts explain the events that eventually led to my uncle's death. Here are some excerpts from Spearhead in the West, which is the 3rd Armored Division's 260-page World War II history published in 1946 as found at www.3AD.com:

> *British forces, driving south from Caen, and American First Army elements, smashing* in an easterly direction, had trapped a sizeable portion *of Field Marshal von Kluge's Seventh Army in the*

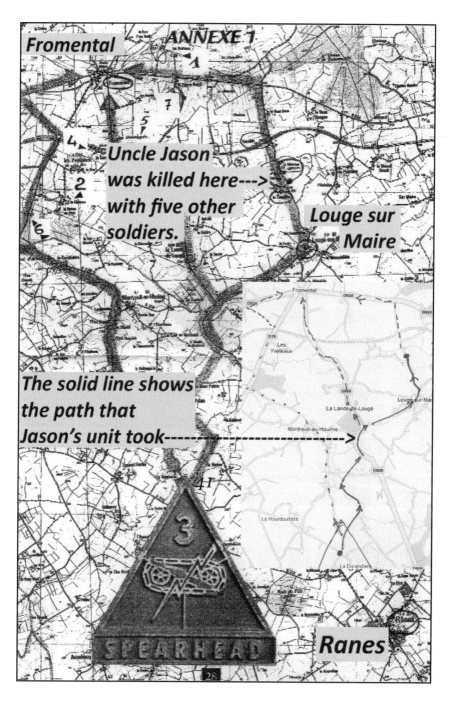

ANNEXE 1

Fromental

Uncle Jason was killed here---> with five other soldiers.

Louge sur Maire

The solid line shows the path that Jason's unit took----------------->

SPEARHEAD

Ranes

'Spearhead' was their nickname due to their fighting style.

Argentan-Falaise pocket. The 3rd Armored Division was ordered to drive deep into this Nazi cauldron of elite units in an attempt to close the escape gap.

Now, the men of the 3rd Armored Division were quiet soldiers, weathered and squint-eyed from the acrid dust of battle. They were schooled in the subtleties of war, their bodies toughened to the sun and the rain and the constant grind of the attack. They were tough, and they knew it. Death was no stranger. Fear was still tangible, but it was honest fear - not the unreasonable panic of those first hours when a man could not distinguish between his own and the enemy's shell fire. It had been a bitter training, but now, the "Spearhead" was a crack team.

(The Third Armored division)...advance ... touched Mayenne, Pre-en-Pail, Carrouges, Ranes, and Fromentel.

...Within hours, the entire combat command would be fighting desperately for its very existence.

(They)...had leaguered in small fields on the outskirts of Ranes, the force was completely

surrounded by the best troops of Nazi Germany - surrounded, and cut off from outside assistance. General Hickey's troops knew this, but they were not overly surprised or alarmed.

Surrounded? Of course - the matter had become a source of pride; the 3rd was always surrounded during its long drives. GI's had begun to chuckle over the division's new watch-word: "Call Me Spearhead," and they expected to be surrounded even as they expected to break out again and go smashing forward to lead the First Army on its next sweep.

Thunderbolt and P-38 Lightning

Overhead, the Thunderbolts and Lightnings of air support strafed and bombed the nearby enemy.

Even beaten, the German soldier at Ranes - Fromentel was good. He was a first class fighting man and troops of the division respected his prowess *as much as they hated his guts.*

At dawn on August 16, the "Spearhead" launched a coordinated attack toward Fromentel. Roads were, for the most part, untenable, and so the task forces used bulldozers and traveled across country.

Jerry assault guns and artillery contested every inch of the route. "Screaming meemies" howled into division forward positions.

Screaming Meemie

A screaming meemie is a rocket launcher. Its name derives from the sound the rockets make when they are fired at the enemy. Even the seasoned soldier would cringe when they announced themselves in flight.

It had been a bitter, fluctuating battle but individual performances were faultless.

On August 17, elements of Combat Command "A" had reached Fromentel from the east while CC "B" was still pinned down by heavy fire on the southwest of town.

The whole battle of RANES-FROMENTEL was close-in fighting with a "Fluid Front." Tanks and tank destroyers had many engagements at ranges less than one hundred yards. Elements of the Division frequently found themselves engaged in stiff fights on ground already passed over by other elements of the Division. The enemy was everywhere, and frequently had no idea where American troops were located; hence, many surprise engagements were fought.

Men of the 3rd Armored Division, resting and repairing their broken equipment, knew that they had faced the best of Germany's fighting forces, and that they had won by a slim margin. They didn't know, or particularly care, that Argentan-Falaise would be a shining name in history.

I have bittersweet thoughts that swing from pride

that my uncle was a part of the 'Spearhead,' one of the toughest outfits in the army, to extreme sadness at our family's loss. On August 17, 1944, the men that approached from the east were my uncle's group, but he was not with them.

Uncle Jason, along with the rest of the 'Spearhead', expected to be surrounded, and they were. They also expected to break through, and they did. However, he and five of his platoon stayed behind as part of the price for victory. They died, along with hundreds more.

According to the testimony of Roger Pillu, he would come along with a friend later that day, August 17, 1944, looking for information about the battle. He would find my uncle and the others, notify an American officer, and later pick up my uncle's helmet. He would hold onto that helmet for sixty years, and for sixty years he would be reminded of the cost of the freedom he so graciously would enjoy.

I would soon be meeting these men who are instrumental in bringing us closer to the unknown. We have always questioned how Jason died, but we knew for certain that he died a hero along with many others.

8

The Sixtieth Anniversary

As I continued through the binder, I came to copies of emails from René that I have saved. I had written an email to René Brideau again asking for more information about the helmet and how it came into the light. Again the translation from French to English was not clear.

TRANSLATION BY COMPUTER (It is not perfect)

Hello Linda,

The helmet of Jason has been found by Roger PILLU where Jason died. He is the last witness living French who saw the bodies of Jason and his friends. He is 89 years old and will be at the ceremony. I think that it is he that will put back the helmet of Jason to Emerson.

Roger PILLU and Arthur LENOBLE (deceased)

found the bodies of Jason and the five other soldiers on the road close to the tank German.

Immediately they warned the unit nearest American. Roger PILLU and Arthur LENOBLE came back at the scene with a Captain American by jeep of the drama. The Captain American removed the six bodies.

Once the Americans left, Roger PILLU noticed that they had forgotten a helmet. He collected the helmet that was the one of Jason. It had the name Barron inscribed on the inside.

Roger PILLU let the helmet in his house and numerous years passed. In 2004 it was the 60th birthday of the landing of Normandy and an exhibition was in the city of BRIOUZE. Each could bring memories of the Second World War. Roger PILLU remembered that he had a helmet American in his house and brought it to the exhibition of the city of BRIOZE.

At this exhibition he met his friend, Roger BIGNON, who was his neighbor during the war. Roger PILLU gave the helmet to his friend, Roger BIGNON.

Roger BIGNON asked people to recover this family American. These people recovered the tomb of Jason at the cemeteries Saint James. Since 2004, every year, Roger BIGNON is going to collect itself on the tomb of Jason at Saint James. In spite of research, no one could find a family who was called BARRON in USA.

Roger BIGNON was in the war of Algeria (1954-1962) with my wife's father. In a conversation he asked me if I could recover this family BARRON in USA. He knew that I had already recovered several families Americans.

In the archives the most recent address (1958) was the one of a Mrs. Hankey. I sent several letters to families HANKEY. One day, I received a message by Internet of Samuel HANKEY that told to me that he knew a member of the FAMILY Barron, Emerson. Samuel HANKEY phoned Emerson.

December 15, 2006 I received your father's letter indicating me the address of Virginia notably.

To the departure, so Roger PILLU had never collected this helmet none of us would have known the place where had died Jason. Jason and his

soldiers arrived at the home of Roger BIGNON.
They died 330 yards of his house.

Cordially
René

Roger Bignon and Roger Pillu

Roger Bignon and Roger Pillu met again during the Sixtieth Anniversary of D-Day. They vowed in 2004 to find the family of Jason H. Barron and return the helmet to them. They had been neighbors in Lougé-sur-Maire during World War II. The helmet was continuing on its journey.

Genevieve and Roger Bignon with René and Marie Antoinette Brideau visiting Jason's grave in Brittany-American Cemetery on the anniversary of Jason's death.

Roger Bignon asked René Brideau to help find Jason Barron's family. Together with their wives, Genevieve and Marie Antoinette, they traveled to Brittany American

Cemetery located in St. James, France, to find Jason's grave and decorate it with flowers. René Brideau was more determined than ever to find the families of the soldiers whose memory continued to touch their lives.

René spent years searching for Jason H. Barron's family and discovering the identities of the five soldiers who died with him. I think he tells it best in an email he sent to us. I have kept the message in the "imperfect translation".

Dear American Friends,

This mail is translated by software of computer. It is not perfected but I hope that you will understand.

The families didn't know the place, or the circumstances of their deaths. During 65 years you could only imagine and could make some suppositions on what had arrived to your dead son in France.

The families first received a telegram of the army American indicating that this soldier was reported missing in action since August 17, 1944 and unfortunately a letter of confirmation of the death will be sent a little later. This letter will indicate merely that this soldier has been killed in action somewhere in France without any other explanation.

Eunice, the woman of Lieutenant Jason BARRON, asked for the information on her husband's death. The army American answered her September 7, 1944:

"I fully understand your desire to learn as much as possible regarding the circumstances leading to his death and I wish there was more information available to give you. Unfortunately, reports as this nature contain only the briefest details as they are prepared under battle conditions and the means of transmission are limited".

In the Archives, I found only one precision indicating that these soldiers have been killed close to the city of Falaise in France. It is merely an indication of the region because they really died to about 16 miles of this city close to the farm of La Métrière in LOUGE SUR MAIRE in the department of Orne in France.

At the time of the battle of Rânes-Fromentel, August 17, 1944, Lieutenant Jason BARRON and his men had just freed the city of Lougé-sur-Maire and headed in the direction of the city of Fromentel. They were suddenly taken under the fire of cannons Germans. The soldiers were at that moment close to a tank German Panther abandoned V (V is the type).

Georges LEFEVRE lived in the farm of La Tirardière that was close to this tank. He had rather passed before this tank a few days and the soldiers Germans in their black uniforms (SS unit) were there. The tank was in breakdown of gas and before leaving the soldiers Germans candle [ignited] some shells of 75 that had not been pulled then on the ditch incendiary [burned the inside of] the tank.

The shells Germans fell and the soldiers Americans tried to protect themselves close to this tank abandoned by the Germans. Sudden a shell hit a big fir tree that was close to them, exploded and killed six soldiers who belonged to the Company F 36th Armored Infantry Regiment at the same time. The other saved soldiers covered their friends with an awning and pursued their attack in the direction of Fromentel.

During these murderous fights, the French

took shelter as they were able to in shelters or trenches that they had dug. Taking advantage of a lull or the cannons didn't pull anymore, Roger PILLU who was 24 years-old and lived also in La Tirardière and his neighbor, Arthur LENOBLE, decided to go to the farm neighboring of La Métrière to see the family BIGNON. Arriving close to the tank German, their attention was attracted by a big awning spread on the road blocking the passage. Intrigued by this camouflage they raised the awning and discovered six soldiers Americans who had died. Horrified by this macabre discovery Roger PILLU and Arthur LENOBLE decided to be going to warn the unit nearest American immediately. When they had arrived to this unit of artillery, they explained to a Captain what they had found on the road.

During this time three other French who were also in La Tirardière, Georges LEFEVRE (17 years), Alphonse VIGEON and Armand CHEVALIER, benefited them also of this lull to leave their shelter. They headed toward the tank German and raised the awning that was on the road. George LEFEVRE tells in his testimony that he will remember all his life what he saw:

> "He had six soldiers Americans who had probably been shredded by a shell. They

*had all their weapons, at least two guns Colt 45
and the rifles. One or two had moved up close to
the tank holding his rifle between the legs, another
had the jagged body. It was not beautiful to see".
The three French put back the awning on the bodies
and continued their path.*

*Roger PILLU and Arthur LENOBLE came back
by jeep with the Captain American at the place of the
drama. The Captain raised the awning, removed
the watch bracelet of one of the soldiers and
gave some orders to remove the bodies quickly.
After their departure, Roger PILLU noted that
the Americans had forgotten two helmets. He
collected the two helmets and took them in his
house in La Tirardière.*

*Maybe two or three days later, Georges
LEFEVRE passed alone close to the tank and found
human remains resting on the side of the road that
began to clear a strong odor:*

> *"He had one forearm, various pieces and a
> hand on which there was a flat alliance (or
> a ring). I remember well of this alliance that
> was of color copper, but that had to be some
> red gold. The hand was inflated so it is
> why I didn't remove the alliance. I was*

surprised that the army American let these human rests and I decided to give them a burial therefore. I went in the field close to the ditch and to about one yard of the stream, between the tank and the stream. I made a hole a little deep with my shovel. These human remains, as well as the alliance, are certainly still where I buried them in 1944 because I don't think that the land was plowed in this place"

Of these five witnesses French, only Roger PILLU (90 years this year) is living. Georges LEFEVRE died in December 2008 and could not attend the ceremony therefore in 2009. Another person, Gilbert BUSE, saw the bodies, maybe, but his testimony is very imprecise and doesn't correspond to those of the other witnesses.

The bodies of the six soldiers were enveloped in sheets and were taken in the cemetery temporary American of GORRON #1 (forty-five miles Northeast of RENNES).

Roger PILLU kept the two helmets then in his house in La Tirardière until 1974 moved in another house in Houlgate in Normandy. During this period, one of the helmets, that didn't have any identification, was lost at the time of works *in his house. There remained therefore only one helmet.*

In 2004, at the time of the 60th anniversary of the landing of Normandy, an exhibition on the Liberation of the canton of BRIOUZE, to which the city of LOUGE SUR MAIRE participated, took place. This exhibition gathered the objects, of the photos of the WWII. Roger BIGNON, who always lived in La Métrière, spoke to Roger PILLU of this exhibition. Roger BIGNON knew Roger PILLU very well because it was his neighbor when he lived in Lougé-sur-Maire. Roger PILLU brought this helmet American therefore at Roger BIGNON and made him gift of it.

Roger BIGNON looked at this helmet and perceived that it had a name, BARRON, and a number inside. He asked a friend of Frédéric BLAIS, Stéphane, who had already done this kind of research, to find the family BARRON. Stéphane found very quickly that Lieutenant BARRON was buried in the Cemetery American of Saint James. But in spite of his research, Stéphane could not find this family American and the years passed (2004, 2005).

In the beginning of the year 2006, my mother-

in-law, Gisèle PIRAUD (Gigi) that was of passage in La Métrière says to Roger BIGNON: "you know, René is going find this family BARRON in USA. I speak of it to him as soon as I arrive at home". Roger didn't believe it at all. I had already recovered some families Americans because my family had rescued May 1st, 1943, Lieutenant Harry ROACH, Navigator of the bombardier B17 N° 42-5780 Black Swan who was dejected by the German hunt close to the German Submarine Basis of Saint Nazaire. The 10 families of this B17 have been recovered with the help of his son Harry Jr. ROACH that lives in Henryville in Pennsylvania.

Nota bene: I don't live in the region of Lougé sur Maire but to 38 miles to the south of the city of NANTES (4:30 to go by car to Lougé sur Maire)

February 10, 2006 I began to look for the family BARRON and I sent a first mail to the A.B.M.C. many other mail will be sent to various places. Some weeks later the first military Archives arrived (the delay could be long, until 24 weeks). Every country to his laws and the laws Americans allows the access these military files to conditions that the soldier died (as Canada, the New Zealand but not the Kingdom United).

Some addresses were notably in the Archives of Lieutenant Jason BARRON. The most recent address (1958) was the one of a Mrs. W. L. HANKEY. I immediately sent several letters to families HANKEY in USA.

December 12, 2006 I received a message of Samuel HANKEY that phoned Emerson BARRON. Just after, Emerson BARRON (brother of Lieutenant Jason BARRON) sent me a letter dated of December 15, 2006. In this letter he indicated me the address of his sister, Virginia McAlister.

Roger PILLU, that collected the helmet of Jason BARRON, sent me his testimony in January 2007.

February 26, 2007 I received a letter of Virginia. We exchanged several letters and photos in all confidence.

I was very happy to have recovered this family BARRON and history could have stopped at that moment. I could not resist the desire to recover these other soldiers Americans of which Roger PILLU had spoken. I continued therefore to look for the information on this history to recover these soldiers.

Roger BIGNON spoke to me of a person that I didn't know, Frédéric BLAIS, which had photographed the helmet of Jason BARRON because he wrote a book on the helmets Americans. Roger BIGNON tells Frédéric BLAIS that I had recovered the family BARRON. A little later, Frédéric BLAIS asked me if I could give him some photos to put in his book. September 3, 2007, with the authorization of Virginia McALISTER, I gave to Frédéric BLAIS documents and photos (the book was published in January 2008).

December 12, 2007 I recovered in the city of Marseille another very important witness Georges LEFEVRE. In his testimony Georges LEFEVRE was categorical: had six soldiers Americans of killed on the road (Roger PILLU was not very sure five or six).

At the end the month of December 2007, Frédéric BLAIS, was going to see Roger BIGNON that showed him my research on these soldiers Americans. Roger BIGNON immediately phoned me to tell me that Frédéric BLAIS was indeed very interested by my research.

December 30, 2007, I received a first message of Frédéric BLAIS. Immediately we understood that we were interested in the history of the WWII and that it was necessary that we work together to identify the five other soldiers Americans.

The work of research was extremely difficult. Indeed, I found no Military Archive mentioning the presence of five soldiers killed with Lieutenant Jason BARRON. It was necessary to find five soldiers killed August 17, 1944 of the Company F.

With Frédéric, we led these researches in parallel. Frédéric had the help of a friend American and a Frenchman who were very effective. Steve BORTS drew up the list of those killed in F company and Emmanuel DELAVILLE brought his aide to determine some dates of death.

In May 2008 we had identified the five soldiers, but was this any good? For example, I received Frédéric's message one evening: "one has a small worry that is going to give us work!"

Records at Gorron indicated there was a soldier named, Robert A. Kennedy buried between Guidry and Hudson. The procedure was to bury soldier in the order in which they arrived at the cemetery. Therefore it was possible that Kennedy died with the soldiers August 17!"

Then some days later: "information arrived stating Robert A. Kennedy died August 10, 1944. He would not have gone therefore with our soldiers to Lougé-sur-Maire!"

I wrote to defers centers of archives: ABMC, Alexandria, Saint Louis, Association 3AD, Cemeteries, Military Historical Institute, NARA, University of the Tennessee, asked for the "morning reports" of the F company for August 17 and 18, 1944 and a lot of other demands.

The military files of soldiers GUIDRY, HUDSON and KOEPL burned at the time of the fire of July 12, 1973 to Saint Louis. It is unfortunately the case of several hundreds of soldiers Americans. http:// www.archives.gov/st-louis/militarypersonnel/fire-1973.html

Then the lists of the deaths exhausted themselves and there were no other soldier of the Company F killed this August 17, 1944 thanks to the code of the cemetery of GORRON, found by Emmanuel DELAVILLE. It is indeed a great luck. We had found the five soldiers who were with Jason BARRON.

I must make homage in Houda, Frédéric's wife, and to Marie-Antoinette, my wife, who have "supported" us during the long hours passed before our computers.

In July 2008, Linda BARRON HEINRICH, at the time of one journey in Europe, went to Saint JAMES and asked the Superintendent of the cemetery Saint James if it was indeed possible that a French possessed her Uncle's helmet 64 years after his death. The Superintendent confirmed that it was indeed possible.

September 6, 2008, Linda sent me a message followed September 23, 2008 of another message to tell me that Jason's family would come for the helmet in France.

I phoned Roger BIGNON and the Mayor of LOUGE SUR MAIRE to ask if it was possible to make a ceremony to the memory of these six soldiers Americans because the family of Lieutenant Jason BARRON was going to come in France. The Mayor accepted and the organization of the ceremony began.

During this time, I continued my research and

thanks to the military archives (notably the address of the cemetery) I recovered the family of David WILLIAMS. Kristopher BILBREY sent me a message November 16, 2008.

December 27, 2008 I went to LOUGE S U R MAIRE because there was a meeting with all those that had to organize this ceremony of Saturday, May 23, 2009. Each gave their opinion on the presentation of the plaque with the names of the soldiers.

We were now in the beginning of the year 2009 and I didn't have the time to look or the four families GUIDRY, HUDSON, KOEPL and PRICE.

Indeed at the same time I made some research and I had recovered to the United Kingdom, the unique sister of the pilot of bombardier Lancaster of the RAF who collapsed, April 2, 1943, before the house where I am born. The 7 flight attendants had been killed. The English family came and a ceremony was organized Sunday, April 2009 5 (an identical ceremony in LOUGE SUR MAIRE) in the region where I lived.

February 7, 2009, I decided to transmit to

Linda BARRON HEINRICH, with whom I had many contacts, the information that I had found in the Archives of theArmy American (addresses of people, of cemeteries and other information) for these families.

I don't know if other families will come in France, it can be next year, in 10 years, in 20 years. By an example, we recovered the 10 families Americans of bombardier dejected B17 May 1st, 1943. The ceremony took place in October 1984 with the family American of which my father had rescued the Navigator, then a second family came in 1985, another in 1997 and the last for the meantime in 2007. It is to say that the time doesn't count.

Know that the inhabitants of the region of LOUGE SUR MAIRE, especially those that knew the war won't ever forget these six soldiers Americans who died for our Liberty. Of the 13 to August 18, 1944, at least 144 American soldiers gave their life to free the region of Rânes-Fromentel. The distance between these two cities is only six miles.

Cordially,
René

In partnership with René , another young Frenchman was researching the soldiers of Lougé-sur-Maire. Frederic Blais, who is in his early thirties, is a historian as well. He had grown-up in the area of Normandy. Here is Frederic's account of his search for the unidentified soldiers:

On 08/17/1944, Roger Pillu picked up the helmet of First Lieutenant Jason H. Barron where the six soldiers were killed in Lougé-sur-Maire, near the Panther tank.

In 2004, Briouze made a show about WWII in the area. All towns from the Briouze County were asked to gather objects and photos of WWII. They also asked me to display some military artifacts (I already did it on my own in Briouze in 1999). Roger Bignon spoke about this "WWII chase" to Roger Pillu and that's how First Lieutenant Barron's helmet re-appeared. The helmet was supposed to be displayed at the show but Roger Bignon chose not to do it. He asked a friend of mine, Stephane, to find the family of the owner of this helmet. Stephane is well known in the area because he searches (and finds) families of pilots whose planes crashed in Normandy. Stephane found very quickly that First Lieutenant Barron is buried in Saint James Cemetery. In the meantime,

I went to see the helmet at Roger's home. Stephane was searching for the family, there was no need interfering in his research, but in fact, he left down the research very quickly.

Roger later asked René about this research and René got in touch with Jason's sister, Virginia, in December 2006.

When my buddy, Regis, and I were working on the helmet book, I obviously chose to display First Lieutenant Barron's helmet because it is a great object itself and moreover it has a great moving power. I went to see Roger to ask his permission and he told me the family of First Lieutenant Barron had been found by René Brideau.

I got in touch with René, who provided the photos published in the book, with the permission of Virginia. I wanted a caption as complete as possible, so I found a website on the internet about the 36th AIR. http://36thair3ad.homestead.com /36AIR_MainPage.html

The webmaster, Steve Borts (Fambor@ aol.com), told me Jason was from Fox Company. Please note the caption in the book tells there were four other men killed alongside Jason. It is based on Roger Pillu's memoirs. The one of George Lefevre, collected by René, telling there were five other soldiers, was far more accurate. The caption was shortened by the publisher, and he cut off the part in which Jason's Silver Star is mentioned... a shame.

The book was published in January 2008. I gave René and Roger Pillu and Roger Bignon each a copy for their precious help.

René called me back later about how I found that Jason was from Fox Company. He told me about the visit of Jason's family in 2009 and the will of the people of Lougé-sur-Maire to inaugurate a plaque for these six heroes. I offered my help, there was little hope that such a task could be fulfilled, but it had to be tried.

I called Steve Borts again for help and he provided me with a list of Fox Company KIAs. Let's call it List 1. There are 120 fallen GIs. The list doesn't mention the dates of death, only names, ranks and serial numbers, but it is the start of everything and Steve must be thanked for this first link in the chain. Steve served in the 36th AIR in the 70s in Germany.

I cross checked with the honor roll on the wesite: http://www.3ad.org/honor_ roll/ listwwiifull.asp. Some days of death are given on this list (List 2) and, in crossing List 1 and List 2, I found two names: PFC Koepl and PFC Price.

The days of death of about 50 soldiers from List 1 were not given by List 2. Therefore the three other soldiers killed in Lougé-sur-Maire were among them and they had to be found.

I then asked my buddy Emmanuel for help. He is a real genealogy wizard on the internet and already performed a lot of great researches. This kind of research was new for him and he knew it would be very hard, but he agreed to try. Emmanuel spent weeks on this research and reduced the missing days of death in list 1 from 50 to 22, and found two more missing soldiers killed on 08/17/44: PFC Hudson and Pvt Williams. But Emmanuel was stopped cold and one name was still missing.

I then started everything from the beginning and found a strange thing: S/Sgt Guidry, was listed KIA on 08/17/1945. That must be a mistake, the German were defeated in August 1945. I cross checked with the honor roll on the wesite: Emmanuel and René checked my theory and found it was 1944, not 1945. George Lefevre told René about the weapons the six dead soldiers had and there were two Colt .45 pistols. Such weapons were only supplied to officers and non-commissions. With the finding of S/Sgt Guidry, everything matched, because we had one Colt for First Lieutenant Barron (officer) and one for S/Sgt Guidry (NCO).

So, we had six soldiers from Fox Company who were KIA on 08/17/1944, but, were there more? Days of death of 22 F Company soldiers were still missing and some of them may have been killed that day, and René checked my theory and found it was 1944, not 1945. George Lefevre told René about the weapons the Emmanuel found a very smart trick during his research. Deceased soldiers were temporarily buried in cemeteries and each cemetery had a specific code. Temporary cemeteries were "following" the front, so each of them is related to a specific area and period, a soldier killed in Belgium in late 1944 was never buried in a cemetery in Normandy where soldiers fell during the Summer of 1944. Emmanuel found a list of KIA soldiers during WWII (List 3) showing such codes. The six soldiers we had found (Barron, Guidry, Hudson, Koepl, Price, Williams) had the same code on List 3, the code of Gorron Cemetery. None of the 22 soldiers whose days of death were unknown had this code. So, none of these 22 soldiers were killed in the same area. That means Fox Company lost "only" six soldiers that day, all near the Panther tank.

I am very grateful to Steve Borts and Emmanuel Delaville, because they helped a lot doing something that seemed impossible at the beginning. Without their knowledge and skills, nothing would have been possible. They deserve much credit.

Fred

Now we had the names of the five soldiers who died with Uncle Jason on August 17, 1944 at Lougé-sur-Maire, France.

9
The Planning Begins

The Planning Committee

Now that they had found the family of Jason Barron, plans for the events were being made in Lougé-sur-Maire. This photo was taken on December 27, 2008. It is the first meeting to organize the ceremony of May 23, 2009. Beginning on the left is Roger Bignon, René Brideau, Joel Marie, Jacques Cabanne, Frederic Blais, and Mayor Marcel Gautier. Also on the committee is Ginette Pitel. She is not pictured because she is taking the photo. These are a few of the names that would soon become heart-warmingly familiar to me.

The ceremony was growing bigger and bigger, and more and more people were becoming involved. A plaque with the names of Uncle Jason and the five soldiers who died with him would be placed by a war memorial in Lougé-sur-Maire. Everyone had a part in getting ready to honor the families of the young men who had liberated their village. A plaque would be placed and the helmet would be returned to the family, bringing closure to a brother who could never make friends with the nightmare that haunted him.

On the following page in the binder is the invitation that had come via email.

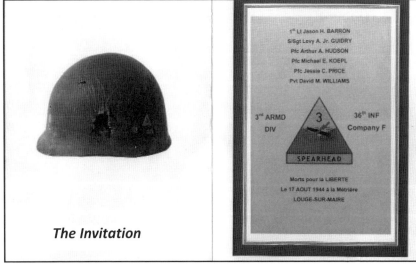

The Invitation

Information written inside of the Invitation:

The war veterans of Lougé sur Maire, Montreuil in Houlme, The Wasteland of Lougé, the Town Council of Lougé sur Maire invite you to the unveiling of a commemorative plaque in honor of six American soldiers who died on August 17th, 1944, in our village.

This ceremony will take place on Saturday, May 23rd, 2009

11 o'clock: Ceremony in the square of Lougé sur Maire which will be followed at the monument where the commemorative plaque for the soldiers will be dedicated.
11: 45 o'clock: Wine of Honor given by the municipality
12:30 o'clock: Luncheon will be served in the Town Hall Dining Room.

On the front was the design of the plaque that would be dedicated in honor of the heroes. On the other side was a picture of Jason's helmet. That helmet with the horrible hole in the side. Why would my father ever want to reclaim this helmet? It would only serve as a reminder of the horrible way Jason died. Was there blood......dried blood that could never be wiped away?

I told our friends, Dave and Debbie Karstaedt, about the helmet and the invitation to go and reclaim it. Dave is a history buff who has researched WWII for years. He tells me, "Go and get the helmet. Even if you put it in a box, keep it in the attic and never look at it, it is part of your family's history."

I read the invitation again. When I saw the names of all six soldiers on the plaque, I thought to myself that it was unfortunate that none of the other families in the United States would know that their loved ones were being honored as well.

If it hadn't been for the fact that I had recently retired, this trip would not have been possible. I worked for the board of education in Washington County as a Staff Development Specialist, and it would have been impossible to get away during the month of May. After thirty-eight years it was a difficult decision to move on to the next phase of my life, but now I feel it was guided by Divine Providence. However, there were other obstacles getting in the way.

As the time grew closer, Dad was becoming an emotional wreck. He cried constantly as I tried to convince him that it was important for him to go. He was 83 years-old with a good mind but wobbly legs. I finally convinced him to go. The next morning when I returned home from shopping there was a note on the door. It simply read, "I'm not going."

As my husband, Brian, put it, "He wants to go, but it's hard to go where the pain is."

Then there was Brian's situation. He was starting a new job and was in limbo. The company kept putting him off about being hired for the position. It was clear that if the job came through he would start immediately. We could not purchase the airplane tickets until he knew about the job. Unfortunately, I had recently become unilaterally deaf and suffered from vertigo. I could not travel by myself in a foreign country. It was looking like we were not going to be able to make the trip. I strongly believed that someone from our family had to be there. It was important to the memory of Jason and it was important to the people of Lougé-sur-Maire.

I started asking people if they could go with me. Everyone had good reasons not to be able to attend. My son who lives in China offered to meet me in France, but he had just begun a new job, working long days. I knew it would be very stressful for him to take off work.

One evening I was writing an email to my nephew and telling him about what was happening in Lougé-sur-Maire. Off the cuff, I wrote, "Wanna go?"

To my delight he replied, "I'll think about it."

I was elated when, the day after I had told him about the ceremony, Ryan called and said, "We are going!"

Ryan is married to a terrific girl named Holly and they have a four-year-old son, Carter. I was overjoyed. Now we could go and fulfill the dream. I was aware that it was very important to the folks in France that someone was there to represent Jason's family. Ryan, who was the oldest Barron grandson of my father, would be keeping the helmet.

It was even better that Ryan and Holly had met in French Class in high school, and could help with communication. Carter was a little gentleman and I knew he would win the hearts of our new French friends. Then Dad decided that since Ryan and his family would be going, he would go also.

I proceeded to make travel arrangements with my friend Alex, a travel agent. The following day I had an email from Ryan. "The economy crisis has hit our company. I don't think we can swing the trip."

The same day Dad had an appointment for a physical at the VA Center. Dr. Brown felt that he should schedule a biopsy for dad. He scheduled it for May 6. Things were looking bleak.

In the next few days Ryan and Holly decided that this was an experience of a lifetime they should not miss. Holly had a special interest in World War II because her grandfather and two great uncles had also served.

Later that week, Brian received a notification that the job placements were not going to be announced until fall so he was now able to go. Things were back on track.

10

The Newspaper Reporter

René had sent me emails weekly to keep me informed of the progress of the memorial ceremonies. He was so sincere and I could tell he was looking forward to meeting us. I began to realize just how big this event was for the people in Lougé-sur-Maire. I sent an email to the local newspaper to ask if they thought there was a story in all of this. A reporter contacted me and we set up an appointment. I told her that if there were going to be photographs, I wanted my father to be included. However, I didn't want him there until I had a chance to give her the information. I knew he would be extremely emotional. She said she would come to my house at 11:00 a.m. and I should tell Dad to come at noon.

When Janet Heim arrived I showed her the binder that I had been keeping with all the information about Jason that I was receiving from France. I said, "Do I have a story?"

She replied, "You have a book."

As I filled Janet in on all that was happening, I could see her interest peaking. At 11:45 a.m. the photographer arrived. He, too, was intent in listening to the story. Then I heard the front door open. Dad appeared in the dining room. The expression on his face told me that he wasn't going to be able to hold it together very long. He seated himself at the table, trembling. Janet spoke to him so kindly, but Dad was unable to answer. I continued giving her information. She took copious notes.

The photographer's heart was also touched. Kevin shot pictures as we continued to relate the story of how the helmet was continuing on its journey. Janet continued to ask Dad questions hoping to give him an opportunity to say what needed to be understood in the article.

Finally he said, "I will tell you. The family suffers."

After that he was able to give Janet some additional information for the article.

Janet took the binder back to the office and studied the contents. She told us that she thought her editor would agree that the story was perfect to be featured on Memorial Day.

As Dad was leaving after the interview, he turned to me and said, "I am going, regardless of what the biopsy reveals."

I hurried and called Alex, our travel agent. "Order our

plane tickets," I told her.

Janet wrote an information packed article. The story was published in The Herald Mail on Memorial Day, May 25, 2009. The story was picked-up by several other newspapers. We received many telephone calls from people who were touched by the story.

Little did I know that this article would eventually be the key to reaching my goal of finding the families of the five soldiers who died with my uncle.

11
Private David Williams
Fentress, Tennessee

Private David Williams
Born in 1923
Fentress, Tennessee
Age at Death: 21
KIA: August 17, 1944
Lougé-sur-Maire, France

I turned to the next page of the binder and read over the names of the other men who would appear on the plaque under Uncle Jason's name:

1st Lt Barron, Jason H.	1920	Somerset	PA
S Sgt Guidry, Levy A. Jr.	1918	Cut Off	LA
PFC Hudson, Arthur A.	1923	Lawrence	TN
PFC Koepl, Michael E.	1913	Chippewa Falls	WI
PFC Price, Jessie C.	1921	Wilbarger	TX
PVT Williams, David M.	1923	Fentress,	TN

There had been some reports in earlier emails that there were five bodies under the awning. Later research showed that there were indeed six mangled bodies under the awning. There was no doubt.

René had mentioned in an email that he had a contact address for the family of David Williams. I decided to write to Kris Bilbrey and tell him about the ceremony. He is the grandson of Pauline, the sister of David.

Kris called me and we had a wonderful conversation. He explained that David had grown up in the hills of Tennessee. The family had since moved to Indiana. Pauline was a toddler when her older brother was killed in action. Kris was very interested in learning more about the circumstances of his great uncle's death.

Although Kris had traveled to Europe several times,

he knew he would not be able to attend the ceremony honoring the fallen soldiers. He was a prosecuting investigator, and there was a huge case that was going to be tried during that time.

Kris and I continued to send emails. I sent him information as I received it. Kris sent me pictures of David Williams' family for my binder. I'm not sure what the word is to describe what I felt when I saw the pictures. Looking at the family who were obviously farmers and probably lived a distance from neighbors, I thought about how close they must have been.

This is a photo of David Williams with his mother and father and all the sisters and brothers. It was taken right after his training before he was sent to Europe. I look at the picture in front of the house and I think to

From left to right: Lorine , Irene , Jack, (little girl is Pauline, Kris's grandmother), David, their mother-Gertie, in front of Gertie is Marvaline, and their father-Paul. Not shown is Sarah, the oldest girl. She is taking the picture.

myself, "This is a story in itself."

The picture of the two brothers, one year apart in age, brought a tear to my eye. David's only brother, Jack, died just last year. I wish he could have known what had happened to his brother, his best friend.

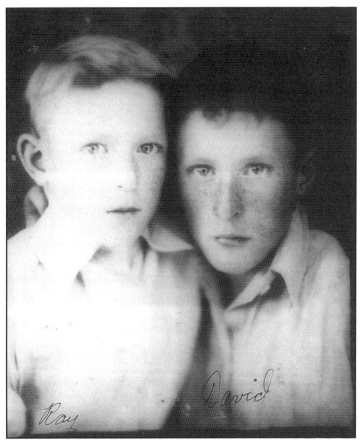

Ray (Jack) and David

Here were two brothers among five sisters. Their ages were 12 and 13. I know they had been great buddies. I can image the adventures they must have had growing up in the Tennessee Mountains.

In the back row are: Irene, Lorine, Pauline (Kris's grandmother) and Marvaline. Sarah and Jack (Ray) are in the front row.

This is a photo of David Williams' sisters and brother. It was taken in 2006. As Kris said, "Everyone is there except David." Here is a message that Kris asked me to read at the ceremony in Lougé-sur-Maire:

> *My name is Kristopher Bilbrey and I am writing on behalf of my grandmother, Pauline Bilbrey (Williams) and her brothers and sisters, as well as, all family and friends of David (D.M.) Williams! We are honored that you have taken time to memorialize these six young men! The commitment they made, not only to our country but to yours, is indescribable!*
>
> *I want to take this time to thank my great uncle David Williams, and the men that gave their*

lives for FREEDOM! If it weren't for men like David, and all men and women that gave their lives in times of conflict... WE WOULD NOT BE WHERE WE ARE TODAY!

It is sad, that David gave his life when it was just starting out. It is always tragic when a young person is lost, but to know that the loss meant something gives the event a bit of meaning!

The part that bothers me so much is that I don't know David... not from stories like I should! See, David was the oldest of his brothers and sisters (who are now older themselves): for example, when he died my grandmother was only three-years-old. One of his sisters and his only brother has now passed on themselves, and my grandmother, just has no real memory of David! I wish I knew his story! From a young age I had known that he was killed in the war but that was it!

However, that does not mean that his sacrifice was in vain... to his family or country! I am proud that David was a military man! I am so glad that he thought enough of his country and helping others that he could do what he did, which is the greatest service anyone could do for their country and freedom! Although I do not "know" David, as a FREE American I KNOW him, and I thank him and the other five that died with him! I also thank their families for the sacrifices they made!

Thank you all and God be with you!

Kristopher H. Bilbrey
United States of America

12
S. Sgt. Levy Guidry, Jr.
Cut Off, Louisiana

S. Sgt. Levy A. Guidry, Jr.
Born in 1918
Cut Off, Louisiana
Died at age 26
KIA: August 17, 1944
Lougé-sur-Maire, France

Late one night, I was sitting at the computer looking up places to visit in France. I thought while we are there we should take a few days and do some sightseeing. It was almost 1:00 a.m. when a thought came to me. If René was able to find the Barron family and get an address for David Williams' family from across the Atlantic, why couldn't I find the families of the other soldiers in the United States? Of course it had been 65 years. Would anyone still be alive? Would anyone care?

It was impossible to get any family information. The Army Archives had burned in St. Louis and all the family information was gone. However, the list that René had sent contained the towns where each of the soldiers had enlisted. I would start there.

Information on Levy Guidry stated that his father lived in Cut Off, Louisiana. I assumed that meant the information had been 'cut off'. I was surprised to learn that his father did indeed live in a town called Cut Off, Louisiana.

I shouldn't have doubted that Cut Off, Louisiana existed. I live in an area called Halfway, Maryland. I often wondered, "What were the founders thinking? Halfway to what?"

The next hours were spent looking up the newspapers in their hometowns. I wrote letters and attached them to emails. An editor responded from Louisiana. She said the attachment didn't come with the email. She suggested that I send it through the mail.

I didn't hear from the other newspaper editors so I decided to send the letter by snail mail to the other newspapers as well.

Here is the letter I sent. In each letter I inserted the name of the deceased soldier and the name of the community that had lost them.

Dear Editor:

During WWII, young members of your community sacrificed their lives so that others could know freedom. I am dedicated to finding the surviving family members of one of the soldiers, Staff Sgt Levy A. Guidry.

He died with my uncle, First Lieutenant Jason H. Barron, born in 1920, Somerset, PA, KIA August 17, 1944 and four other soldiers: PFC Arthur A. Hudson, born 1923, Lawrence, TN; PFC Jessie C. Price, born 1921, Wilbarger, TX; PFC Michael Koepl, born 1913, Chippewa, Wisconsin; PVT David M. Williams, born in 1923, Fentress, TN.

On May 23, 2009, a plaque will be dedicated by the people of Lougé-sur-Maire, France, in appreciation for the part that these young soldiers played in liberating their village.

I will be attending the ceremony. When I return I would like to share this honor with the surviving family members and the people of your community.

Here is the information that I received from the people of Lougé-sur-Maire on Levy A. Guidry, Jr: Date of birth: October 25, 1918, buried in LaFourche Parish, Louisiana, father-Levy Guidry, Sr. Young Levy may have resided in Ft. Lauderdale, Florida.

These men and their families suffered a loss that can never be forgotten. The people of Lougé-sur-Maire have worked hard to find family members. Only the families of my uncle, 1st LT Jason Barron and PVT David Williams have been found. I hope that your readers can help me find the family of Levy A. Guidry. His family deserves to know about this honor.

An engraving on the walls of the bell tower in Brittany American Cemetery, in St. James, France, reads as follows:
> *"As these bells ring,*
> *The honored dead rest,*
> *And freedom lives."*

I included my home address, email address and phone number.

It came to me that I could also write to American Legions, VFW's, and Historical Societies. Time was getting short, but these families had to know about what the people of Normandy were doing to honor the heroes in their families.

Two weeks before I was to leave for France a call came. A southern voice said, "Linda, I understand you are looking for the family of Levy Guidry. I'm calling from New Orleans. My name is Joan Eymard and I am Levy's sister."

My knees went weak. "Joan, I can't believe it. Levy's family was the last family I thought I would find."

"Oh, you heard about our little event here. What you must understand is that after all we have been through here in New Orleans, we are community. We watch out for one another. I have received several phone calls. Your letter was published in our newspaper."

Joan related the story about Levy being stationed in Indian Gap, Pennsylvania, and her mother taking the three sisters on a coal-driven train from New Orleans to spend time with Levy. They stayed together in one room in a hotel. Levy would come and visit in the evening. They stayed there until Levy shipped out. I could hear trembling in Joan's voice as she said she was so sorry her mother was not alive. She had died a few years earlier at the age of 97. Her mother never knew the circumstances relating to her son's death.

The American Legion in Larose, Louisiana, Number 70373 is named for Levy Guidry, Jr. It is called the Gros-Guidry American Legion. These were the first men to be killed from that area in World War II.

Joan mentioned to me about the Higgins boats. This was the name of the boats that landed at the Normandy beaches. They were made there in New Orleans. During the war practically everyone worked on the Higgins Boats.

Higgins Boats

Joan's daughter, also named Joan, and her son, Hilton, began sending emails to me. Hilton went to Levy's tomb and took pictures to send to me. There was the date I was looking for - August 17, 1944.

Joan said that her mother could not bring herself to spend the small death benefit that arrived each month after Levy was KIA. Instead, she bought a mausoleum for his burial and a baptismal font for their church. All the grandchildren in the family were baptized in it.

Levy's stone at his mausoleum

Levy's body was not sent home for a long time, when his remains arrived, someone asked her mother, "What if that isn't your son in that box?"

Her mother replied, "Then I will take care of him and pray that the mother who receives my son will do the same."

Pictures and information that I received about Levy Guidry would inhabit the next twenty pages of my binder.

Two of Levy's sisters were nurses in the military. Nora had passed away and left behind her daughter, Linda, also a nurse. Nancy was 83 years of age and lived in Chicago. Joan was a retired teacher, the same as me.

Pictured is the postcard that Levy wrote to his sister, Nora. Notice the date that it was written - June 6, 1944, D-Day, the day of the Normandy invasion. It is so full of hope. The young soldier was certain that he would soon be going home.

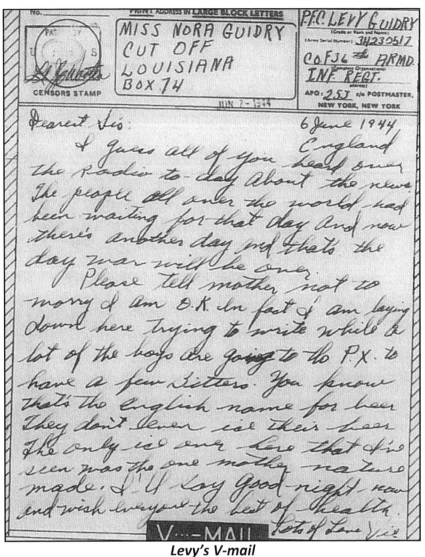

Levy's V-mail

This is what he wrote:

6 June 1944

England

Dear Sis,

I guess all of you heard over the radio about

the news. The people all over the world had been waiting for that day and now there's another day, and that's the day war will be over.

Please tell mom not to worry. I'm O.K. In fact, I'm here laying down trying to write, while a lot of the boys are going to the PX to have a few Bitters. You know that's the English name for beer. They don't even ice their beer. The only ice over here that I've seen was the one Mother Nature made. I'll say good-night now and wish everyone the best of health.

Lots of love,
Levy

On September 3, 1944 the following telegram arrived:

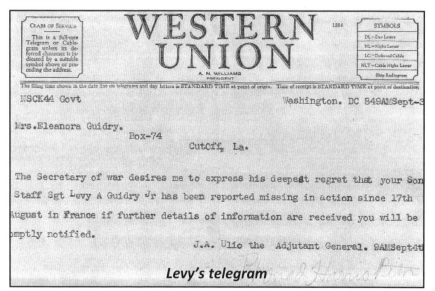

Levy's telegram

This telegram indicated that Levy was missing in action. Shortly after the telegram arrived a follow-up letter was sent from the War Department explaining what the term "Missing In Action" means.

4 September 1944
Mrs. Eleanora Guidry
Box 74
Cut Off, Louisiana

Dear Mrs. Guidry,

This letter is to confirm my recent telegram in which you were regretfully informed of your son, Staff Sergeant Levy A. Guidry, Jr. 34, 230, 517, Infantry, has been reported missing in action since 17 August 1944 in France.

I know that added distress is caused by failure to receive more information or details. Therefore, I wish to assure you that any time additional information is received it will be transmitted to you without delay, and, if in the meantime no additional information is received, I will again communicate with you at the expiration of three months.

The term "missing in action" is used only to indicate that the whereabouts or status of an individual is not immediately known. It is not intended to convey the impression that the case is closed. I wish to emphasize that every effort is exerted continuously to clear up the status of our personnel. Under war conditions this is a difficult task as you must readily realize. Experience has shown that many persons reported missing in action are subsequently reported as prisoners of war, but as this information is furnished by countries with which we are at war, the War Department is helpless to expedite such reports. However, in order to relieve financial worry, Congress has enacted legislation which continues in force the pay, allowances and allotments to dependents of personnel being carried in a missing status.

Permit me to extend to you my heartfelt sympathy in the period of uncertainty.

Sincerely yours,
J.A. Ulio
Major General
The Adjunct General

This telegram and subsequent letter about Levy being missing in action must have been received with a mixture of emotions. There was hope and there was dread. What had they heard of the German treatment of their prisoners? Would he be cared for if injured? If he was healthy would he try to escape? Or would they discover that he had been killed in action after all. There would be no escape from the carousel of second guessing. There could only have been the faintest wisp of hope that Levy would be safe and coming home.

On the day following my initial conversation with Joan, I answered my phone and heard the familiar southern voice saying, "Linda, I'm going to France! I don't have my passport yet, but I'm going!"

Thus began the friendship between the families of Levy Guidry and Jason Barron.

13

PFC Jessie C. Price Wilbarger, Texas

A week passed and I didn't get any more responses to my letters. I don't know why I didn't think about it sooner, but I remembered a list that had some names and vague addresses that René had sent two years ago. The information was from 1947, the year I was born. It was so long ago. Sixty-two years to be exact. I was a true baby-boomer. Surely the people who were named on the list were deceased, or they had moved. Many places had gone to a different system of addresses. Rural roads were now city streets in many cases.

I found the last name of a sister of Jessie C. Price in Vernon, Texas. My husband told me about a program on the computer where I could search for people. I was irritated that he didn't tell me sooner. We searched the internet looking for a Marjorie Henderson somewhere in Texas. There was a list of Hendersons. I saw the name Leon Henderson. I had a feeling this man would somehow be connected. Then I saw Marjorie Henderson, age 82.

The age was right. I knew in my gut that this was Jessie's sister. I hesitated to call. How was I going to start the conversation? I was afraid she would think I was a telemarketer. I had to get a lot of information in before she hung up on me. When I finished there was silence. Then in a sweet Texan voice she said, "I am so happy you found me."

We talked for an hour. She said that Jessie's body, "J.C." as they called him, didn't arrive in the United States for three years.

Marjorie explained to me that several of the siblings were living, but in poor health. She is still very active and is an accomplished seamstress. She was a widow. Leon had died recently after suffering from a stroke. Marjorie had taken care of him for many years. She missed him tremendously. For all that she had been through her voice was very young-spirited and joyful. It was my greatest pleasure to be able to tell her about the honor that was going to be bestowed upon her brother.

Marjorie's sweet daughter, Inez, and I began to correspond through email. Over time I would get to know more and more about the family that shared this tragedy with us.

Over the years I have done a lot of complaining about computers. I now realize that I owe an apology to someone. The story that was about to unravel would have never happened if it were not for modern technology.

The helmet would still be in the attic in Roger Bignon's farmhouse, the families of the brave soldiers would never know how their loved ones were being honored, and my father would still be wondering, "What happened to my brother? Was he alone? Did he suffer? Did anyone care?"

14

PFC Michael Koepl
Chippewa Falls, Wisconsin

I am sure there are at least a dozen people in Wisconsin that think there is a Linda Barron Heinrich in Maryland that is nuts. I searched the internet and wrote to every Koepl in Wisconsin that I could find. Not one person replied.

The day before I was to leave on the trip, a miracle happened. I received a call from Edward J. Nayes. Ed resides in Stanley, Wisconsin. The folks at the American Legion had given him my letter and he was willing to search for the family of Michael Koepl. On the phone, I attempted to fill Ed in on all that was happening. At one point I stopped and ask him a question. There was silence. In a few seconds I heard his trembling voice say, "Give me a minute."

I didn't realize it at the time, but I was going to learn that I was communicating with a true patriot; a man who gave his time preserving the memory of those who had given their lives in defense of our freedom.

He would prove to be a valuable ally in my search. My quest to find the families of all six soldiers was in sight.

I copied the emails from Ed and put them in a sheet protector. This page would represent Michael Koepl. He now had a place in my binder.

15

PFC Arthur A. Hudson Lawrenceburg, Tennessee

I came to the next sheet protector in the binder. I had written "Arthur A. Hudson" in the center of a blank sheet of paper and put it in the sheet protector. I am saving this space for Arthur. Where could his family be? So far, there were no responses to any of my letters. The ceremony would proceed without my knowing the whereabouts of the Hudson family.

I had information that Arthur had a sister named Estelle Methvin. We found several listings of Methvin's on the internet. I wrote letters to all of them inquiring about Arthur and his sister, Estelle. I received one reply saying that they had no knowledge of Estelle or her brother.

I thought that it was curious that one of the young Frenchmen who happened by on that tragic day answered to the same first name as one of the fallen soldiers. Arthur Lenoble would die never knowing this coincidence.

My heart ached to find Arthur A. Hudson. As René would later say, "Linda caught the 'virus'- the good virus of research."

In the back of my mind, I was beginning to fear that I would never find the family of this soldier. No one would ever know that this young hero was still honored by the people he liberated. They would not know that his name is in bright gold letters on the beautiful granite plaque in Lougé-sur-Maire, France. They would not know that the people of Lougé-sur-Maire longed to meet them and express their gratitude to them personally.

Selfishly, I ached for myself. I had been so determine to find all of the families. Now it looked like the circle was not going to be complete.

16

Turbulence

The airplane hit turbulence. The tone sounded for the seatbelts to be engaged. I closed the binder and put my head back waiting for the uneasiness to subside. It had to be pretty important for me to cross the Atlantic in an airplane. The helmet invaded my thoughts. Yes, it was very important.

After some time, the turbulence settled and the plane hummed along smoothly.

The Barrons are a patriotic family. My father never missed an opportunity to tell anyone who would listen about how proud he was to be an American. He complained that the young people didn't care about the sacrifices that were made for the freedom they enjoyed. They didn't understand that they could lose their freedom at any time. In all fairness, how could they understand? A war had never been fought on our homeland during their life time.

The events of 9-11 were a hint of what could happen. It was a burp in American history.

As a result of my dad's patriotic spirit, I, too, am very patriotic. It irritates me when I am working at the concession stand at my sons' sporting events and during The Star-Spangled Banner, people continue to order food and the other parents continue to serve them. I was at a meeting where it was discussed if we even needed to continue playing the national anthem. I made my feelings known.

I have a vision in my mind that has never left my memory. Years ago, my husband and I were entering a park where a festival was being held. There was a military band playing on a stage across the way. Suddenly they started playing the national anthem. My husband and I stopped walking and faced the military band. Everyone else continued as they were, looking at the crafts, ordering food, and talking to their friends. But there was a man that caught my eye. Amongst all the people meandering around, there stood a man in bib overhauls in the middle of the field. He was standing at attention with his hand on his heart. To me, it was a Norman Rockwell picture.

How did we reach this point? Why do we take our freedom for granted? Just like the turbulence in the air, I believe that unless we learn to value our freedom, there is going to be rough-riding ahead.

Part II

"The Spoken Language is difficult to understand, but the Language of the Heart is loud and clear."
Linda Barron Heinrich

17

Sacred Memorials

We made it! We landed in London and enjoyed the sights for two days. Then we took the train through the tunnel, under the English Channel, to France. We rented a van and we were on our way. We spent our first night in Le Havre, Normandy. We were seeing many reminders of the war that had occurred there many years before. The land was very flat. It was clear why this was the area that the Germans had chosen to march across.

I was becoming very apprehensive. What will the French people think of us? How will we communicate? How is Dad going to hold up? I've always heard that the French people don't like Americans. Did I do the right thing by insisting that we come? It was a bit late to second guess myself, but I suppose it is natural. So far we were enjoying the trip, yet dad seemed to only give partial attentions to the landmarks we visited.

Several times during the planning of the trip and

since landing in Europe, I had the feeling that someone was watching over us, even guiding us. This feeling was very strong now. This feeling would visit me many times during the trip.

After a restful night's sleep, our first stop was the Normandy Cemetery and Memorial at Omaha Beach. Originally, we had planned to stop at Mont St. Michel, but as we drove past the signs to Omaha Beach we decided this was more important. We needed to be in Lougé-sur-Maire by evening. We were to have dinner at the Bignon Farm that night.

My dad became very melancholy, often withdrawing into himself. From the first moment we approached the memorials from the parking lot, there was a sense of the sacred. Everybody whispered in hushed tones. There was stillness and a reverence that permeated the air.

We walked down the path toward the English Channel in what seemed like an endless parade of people. We passed a plaque that was engraved with information that indicated that we were on grounds that had been given to the United States. It reminded me that those who were buried in France were in American soil.

The next building was a museum. We did not enter at this time, but we did notice a pool with a small waterfall at the end of it. Inside the basement level, we would later find displays and films of the personal stories of many fallen soldiers.

Museum at Normandy Cemetery and Memorial

Anticipation built as we approached a turn in the sidewalk that would take us closer to the beaches. We had seen them in movies and documentaries about the war, but this was the real thing. We were finally there.

We caught our first glimpse of Omaha Beach. It was easy to see why it was chosen as a landing place for the invasion to take place with its long, flat beaches and what seemed like a shallow water approach. You could see the sandy bottom far into the channel.

Dad was as quiet as ever. We stopped to take a couple of pictures, while he sat on the wall. I didn't need to imagine what my dad was thinking. I knew.

It was breath-taking. I marveled at the tranquility. As I looked out over the beach, it seemed surreal, the water was so blue. The grounds were beautiful and neatly groomed. Hundreds of people strolled among the more than 10,000 White Crosses and Stars of David. I stopped to listen to the birds as they sang unaware of the ravished land that stood here 65 years ago. How on earth could this have been the place of so much death and destruction?

Emerson reflects as the waves of Omaha Beach splash in the distance.

I always keep a journal when traveling. Here is my entry for May 22, 2009:

> *Today has become a day that will be engraved in my memory. We slept in, had breakfast, and then started for Omaha Beach and the Normandy Cemetery and Memorial. I cannot find words to describe the blue of the water as we stood on the cliffs and looked out over the channel. The memorial*

and the gardens are far more sacred and beautiful than I could have imagined. There were thousands of people honoring the sacrifices made for freedom. At the memorial a lady thanked Dad for his sacrifice for our freedom. The weather is perfect! Blue sky, gentle breeze, sunshine, vivid green foliage everywhere, cliffs, and the poppies grow.....

This day didn't go as I had planned. It was so much better.

We walked along quietly listening to accents of the different nationalities also visiting. The majority of them were French, or so it seemed, with a few Asian, American and British. We continued to a reflecting pool that led to a monument with a statue in the center. While we were there, bells chimed beautiful patriotic songs. "America, the Beautiful" played as we were preparing to leave.

The side rooms depict the European and Pacific Campaigns.

I gazed back at the horrendous number of crosses. I realized the magnitude of lives lost, but, beyond that, the number of mothers, fathers, children, wives, girlfriends, brothers, sisters, and friends that were affected by each death was unimaginable.

The cemetery reminded me of Arlington Cemetery back in the states.

As my father sat on a bench reflecting, a woman took notice of him. She must have understood the sadness on his face. The age was right. Surely, he had been a veteran. Perhaps he had landed on this beach sixty-five years ago.

She sat down beside him and spoke to him in her French-Belgium accent. They shared stories. Her father had been part of the underground in Belgium. He had helped many Jewish people escape to England.

Before leaving, she shook my father's hand
and thanked him for his sacrifice.

If I had my way, every person who has lost a family member or friend in World War II, or every person who has an interest in the war, would be able to visit these hallowed grounds. It would be an experience far beyond their imagination or dreams.

On the way out to the parking lot, we went into the museum. People continued to talk in hushed tones as they walked through reading the many displays of individual heroism and valor. There was a film that reflected on the many soldiers that sacrificed for pride and honor, but mostly for their comrades. In a larger theater it gave an overview of the cemetery, D-day, and many testimonials of survivors of that bloody day.

On the upper level, you have a view of the English Channel beyond the pool that seems to blend in with the sea. On the nearest edge of the pool was a diagram of the Normandy invasion showing the code names of the troops and landing zones. It was only the beginning of the honors that the American and French governments would display for the soldiers who had paid the ultimate sacrifice.

The English Channel seems to reach into the museum.
The near edge shows the beach landings.

Next, we went to Brittany American Memorial Cemetery in St. James. Here was the resting place of my uncle. The summer before I had briefly visited my uncle's grave. I had gone to Oxford, England, to visit my son who was a student there. I asked him to take me to St. James.

While there, Supt. Arseneault introduced us to another group of people who were visiting. One was a World War II veteran who had traveled from the United States with his son to France to visit several gravesites. He was one of the few in his company that had survived the D-Day invasion. He had come to visit his buddies who were laid to rest here in the cemetery. We shook hands, and then I felt the urge to reach out and hug him. He returned the hug and I felt his body tremble.

As I left the peaceful grounds, I turned and said good-bye. I would not be returning again, or so I had assumed. Life holds many uncertainties.

Now, it is a year later. Supt. Gerald Arseneault greeted us at the office. I had sent him an email stating that we would be visiting my uncle's grave on Friday, May 22, 2009. He grabbed the bucket of damp Omaha Sand that he would use to make the engraved letters stand out. Dad's legs grew weak and the superintendent offered him a ride on a golf cart that was nearby for that very reason. Dad refused a ride and led the procession toward the chapel. He remembered the general direction from a visit ten years earlier with his grandson, my son, Brent.

Supt. Arseneault asked my nephew to bring a chair

for his grandfather. He guided us to the cross bearing Jason's name. I looked at his name and thought, "While the rest of us have been living our lives, you have been here all that time."

Resting place of our hero.

The superintendent explained that they used the sand from Omaha Beach because it would not stain the stone and would fall away clean when it dried. The engraved letters stood out. He told us that each soldier received a military burial and that a minister of their faith oversaw the service.

Dad was asked, "Would you like it if 'Taps' was played?"

He replied, "Yes....very much."

Everyone stood quietly facing Jason's cross, each

with their hand over their heart. The superintendent saluted. Dad would remind us many times afterwards how important that moment was to him.

The superintendent asked us if we had any questions. He told us interesting details about the cemetery. It was easy to see that he cared about the soldiers and their families. He then left us with Jason. I showed Carter the name "Barron" on Jason's cross and he whipered, "That's my name."

Emerson rests with his brother and answers Ryan's questions about the service and ranks.

We went into the bell tower. Looking out over the 4410 graves, the impact of the war set in. As I descended through the tower, I noticed a plaque engraved with these words:

> *"as these bells ring,*
> *honored dead rest,*
> *liberty lives."*

All of the five men who died with Uncle Jason had been exhumed and sent to the United States for permanent interment. I never understood why Jason wasn't brought home. It was done at the expense of the United States government, so money wasn't the issue. The decision would have been made by my grandparents and Eunice. They were gone, so we will never know the answer.

View from the church tower. The eagle at the top of the flag pole marks the location of Uncle Jason's grave which is blocked by the tree.

But here he was. He was with more than 4,400 men, including 22 sets of brothers buried side by side. Ninety-seven of the crosses marked the graves of unknown soldiers. On the retaining wall of the memorial terrace are inscribed the names of 498 of the Missing whose resting place "is known only to God." These men had fought for a common cause. Here he was in this beautiful setting, visited by those who had an overwhelming feeling of pride for what these soldiers had accomplished. We were told that people in the surrounding villages adopted grave sites and brought flowers to decorate them. Some prayed for the families. I later learned that Roger and Genevieve Bignon along with René and Marie Antoinette Brideau made a pilgrimage to St. James cemetery every year on August 17. They put flowers on Jason's grave just as, Denise, the sister of Roger Pillu, had placed flowers on the site where the six soldiers had been killed.

Dad was at peace. I was at peace. Jason was where he belonged.

Emerson gives his brother a final salute.

18
The Bignon Farm

Linda, Carter and Emerson at the farm.

We were invited to have dinner on Friday evening at Roger Bignon's farm. We were running late. We arrived at the Bed and Breakfast in Ranes where Roger Bignon had reserved rooms for us. The innkeeper called Roger Bignon to tell him we had arrived. René, Frederic and Lea, Stephane's daughter, drove to meet us and lead us to the farm. I was so happy to meet René. We have emailed each other for over two years. We looked at each other like we had so much to say, but he speaks no English and I speak no French. We looked at each other and laughed.

Roger and Genevieve Bignon come out to greet us.

When I first met Frederic I wasn't quite sure who he was. I had not made the connection that he was the author of the book on helmets. Fortunately, Frederic speaks fluent English. I would soon learn that he was a major force in getting these events off the ground. Soon we were on our way from the Inn to the Roger Bignon's farm. Roger has had the helmet in his possession for the last five years. Driving up the tree lined lane, we approached the farmhouse. I was in awe of the tranquility, the neatly trimmed lawn, the colorful flowers, and the stately hedges. We got out of the van. Roger and Genevieve Bignon came down the steps to greet us. They were followed by their son, Stephane and his wife

Valerie. Valerie also speaks English. What a relief! Next Marie Antoinette, René's wife, comes down the steps with her mother, Gigi. I am struck by the beauty of these people.

There is a period of quiet. Then standing at the top of the steps I see Joan. She is slim and trim and has lovely white hair. She is a youthful 72 years of age. We do not speak. She descends the steps as I begin to climb. We embrace in a hug while our French friends watch. They must have felt a certain amount of pride knowing they are responsible for this meeting. Joan moves on to my father and they embrace, and the tears begin to flow. They share a common bond, something they did not ask for, something they did not want, but nonetheless, it was something that had a major impact on their lives.

Joan's husband, Hilton, extends his hand in friendship. In two short weeks they had obtained their passports, made travel arrangements, and arrived in France in tip top shape to take part in honoring the memory of Joan's brother.

There is a moment of awkward silence. As I turn around, out of the corner of my eye, I see Carter trip and fall. He cut his head on some gravel. Everyone swings into action and we move into the farmhouse. Marie Antoinette offered her hand to Carter. He took it, and together they walked up the steps. Marie Antoinette took care of the cut and Carter was happy once again.

I haven't said much about Carter. At four years of age he can engage in a conversation, but he is not precocious. He is very sweet. He has added so much to this trip. He says "bonjour" and "merci" and smiles at everyone. He is the hope of the future. Perhaps the experience he shares with us will in some way influence the future of our nations.

The American flag was placed at the entrance to the farm to welcome Jason Barron's and Levy Guidry's families.

Sixteen people sit around the table in the comfortable farm kitchen. Seven delicious courses are served including lots of homemade wine. I believe that Roger has made the best wine I have ever tasted. Later he offers us cognac that he made twenty years ago. I take a whiff and instantly know I cannot handle it.

Joan and Hilton are keeping the conversation lively with their Cajun French. During this time, a lot of misconceptions are cleared up. There were several things that I was mistaken about due to the imperfectly-translated French on our emails.

Seated from left to right are: Houda and Frederic Blais, Brian, Valerie and Stephane Bignon, Joan and Hilton Eymard, Genevieve Bignon, Marie Antoinette Brideau, Roger Bignon, Gigi (peeping over Roger's shoulder), René Brideau, Linda, Emerson Barron, and Ryan Barron. Holly is taking the picture and Carter is sleeping on the sofa nearby.

Holly and Ryan are practicing their French on our new friends and doing very well. Carter is drinking orange juice from a little liqueur glass. Soon he is weary and goes over and falls asleep on the sofa. There was so much talking and so much laughter. I need not have worried about communication. I think to myself, "The spoken language is difficult to understand, but the language of the heart is loud and clear. "

I sit back and relax. I am overcome with abundant gratitude for these people, the people of Normandy.

At midnight the decision is made that we should go to bed. Everyone is staying at the Bignon farmhouse, except us. Since my husband snores so loudly it rattles the windows, we are staying at the Bed & Breakfast in Ranes. Tomorrow is a very big day.

Hilton and Roger are touring the farm.

Here are a few of our new friends:
Marie Antoinette, René, Lea, Stephane and Valerie on the farm.

19
The Dedication

Church in the center of Lougé Sur Maire.
The plaque is at the base of the war memorial to the right.

I had assumed that the ceremony would be small. After all, the village was very small. There would be a few words said, the plaque would be unveiled, we would accept the helmet, we would have lunch and then we would wait around until Sunday's ceremony in Gorron. Well, I was in for a surprise.

When we arrived in Lougé-sur-Maire, I was amazed at the number of people standing near the church. They had come from all over the area. This was a huge event. The church was magnificent.

The day was slowly turning gray as a rain-storm was approaching. We were ushered over to the church where we were greeted by Mayor Gautier. I heard stirring patriotic music coming from the church. People began walking into the church. My family and Joan's family were led to the center of the courtyard in front of the church. Many introductions were made. The mayor was holding a large arrangement of flowers. Men were standing in a semi-circle bearing large colorful flags. I counted them. There were sixteen in all. The media was snapping shots. I have never had so many cameras flashing at me.

Now it was time for the procession to begin. First, Mayor Gautier walked into the church and placed flowers on the altar. Sixteen flags representing the communities of the area were then carried in by men. They encompassed the front of the church. Next, we were led into the church followed by a group of children. The congregation rose and we were marched to the front. I immediately noticed the sacred splendor of the centuries old building. I am in awe of the grandeur - the magnificence of this ceremony. I take notice of the framed military pictures of my uncle and Levy Guidry on the table at the altar. The picture of Levy is one that I had received from Joan's niece, Linda Bienvenue. My husband had scanned it into the computer and sent it to René.

A group of children followed us and sat to the front right of us. Next I noticed a group of young musicians playing the beautiful music that was giving me cold chills. They were seated to the front left. The music stopped.

The inside of the church is majestic.

Roger Bignon stood up and went to the front of the church. In the beautiful French language he read the following:

Dear Friends,

   During the battle of Ranes-Fromentel, six American soldiers were killed by a shell on August 17, 1944 near La Metriere in Lougé-sur-Maire. They belonged to F Company, 36th Armored Infantry Regiment.

1st Lt Barron, Jason H.	*Age 23*	*Somerset, PA*
S Sgt Guidry, Levy A. Jr.	*Age 25*	*Cut Off, LA*
PFC Hudson, Arthur A.	*Age 21*	*Lawrence, TN*
PFC Koepl, Michael E.	*Age 31*	*Chippewa Falls, WI*
PFC Price, Jessie C.	*Age 22*	*Wilbarger, TX*
PVT Williams, David M.	*Age 20*	*Fentress, TN*

   These soldiers were discovered on the road, near a German Panther tank, by Roger Pillu and Arthur Lenoble and then by George Lefevre, Alphonse Vigeon, and Armand Chevalier. Roger Pillu and Arthur Lenoble contacted the nearest American unit and came back with a Captain. This Captain then organized the collecting of the bodies, but for an unknown reason, the helmets were left on the ground. Roger Pillu, who lived at la Tirardiere in Lougé-sur-Maire, picked up two of these helmets and kept them. In 2004, during the 60th anniversary of the Normandy landings, Roger Pillu gave this helmet to me. This helmet reappeared thanks to an exhibition about the liberation of the Briouze County, in which the town of Lougé-sur-Maire took part.

During a conversation, I asked René Brideau, who has a great interest in history and had already contacted American families, if he could find the family of the soldier to whom this helmet belonged. The helmet only had a name and an Army Serial Number. After researches in the US Army Archives and many letters sent, René Brideau found the family in December 2006.

First Lieutenant Barron was married, his wife was named Eunice. He was from a big 9-children family. Jason had 5 brothers and 3 sisters. They lived in Somerset, Pennsylvania. Today only remains one brother, Emerson, who lives in Maryland, and one sister, Virginia, who lives in Florida. Jason H. Barron rests in peace in Saint-James Military Cemetery.

In his memories, George Lefevre was positive

there were 6 dead American soldiers on the road.

Then, the names of the 5 other soldiers, killed alongside Lieutenant Barron, had to be found. René Brideau and Frederic Blais, who is also interested in history, lead researches, helped by American and French friends. Steve Borts gave the complete list of Company F dead soldiers and Emmanuel Delaville was of great help to determine some days of death. The five other soldiers were found in the process, after a long research, the 5th being Staff Sergeant Guidry.

Private David M. Williams lived in Muncie, Indiana, and had 5 sisters and one brother. He is buried in Elm Ridge Cemetery, in Muncie. His family was found in November 2008.

Staff Sergeant Levy A. Guidry Jr. lived in Cut Off, Louisiana. Levy had three sisters: Nora and Nancy, both Military nurses during WWII, and Joan, who is among us today. Levy is buried in Cheramie Cemetery. His family was found less than 15 days ago.

Private Jessie C. Price lived in Vernon, Texas. His family was found 8 days ago. In the future, families of Privates Price and Williams will come to Lougé-sur-Maire and researches go on to find families of Privates Hudson and Koepl.

Without Roger Pillu, who picked up this helmet, American families would have never known where these six soldiers were killed. U. S. Army Archives only state they were Killed in Action in Falaise, France. From August 13th to August 18th, 1944, at least 144 American soldiers gave their lives to liberate the Ranes-Fromentel area.

Thank you for your attention.

After he returned to his seat, the congregation raised their voices in a beautiful French hymn. The orchestra played. Roger Bignon sang out. Later we would learn that several members of the orchestra were his relatives. They were a very musical family. The service continued for a little over half an hour of brief speeches and songs.

At the conclusion, we were led in a slow procession outside and around to the side of the church. I hadn't noticed the statue of the soldier when I was waiting outside before the ceremony. Chairs were lined up in front of the statue.

We were motioned to be seated, as people continued to pour out of the church. More than a hundred villagers were standing behind us.

*Mayor Gautier prepares to place the flowers
at the plaque.*

Frederic looked up and around as though he was concerned that the sky was about to open at any second and we would be drenched. It didn't matter to me. As the gentle raindrops began to fall, I thought it was quite appropriate for the occasion. Frederic began with his speech. Others spoke as well. My eyes were fixed on the American Flag that was spread out at the foot of the statue.

We were handed English copies of the speeches as they were made. How very kind! They thought of everything. Dad and Joan were signaled to come forward by the mayor.

The mayor handed Dad and Joan each a ribbon attached to the corners of the flag. They pulled on the ribbons and the flag slowly uncovered the treasure below. It was the plaque. I heard myself gasp. The orchestra started playing the anthems of the two nations as we stood at attention. The names flew out to me in bright gold against a granite background. These were the names. The names of the soldiers I had dedicated the last few weeks to finding. They were my reason for being here. I must find their families. They must know what happened here today.

Joan and Emerson uncover the plaque.

The inscription at the bottom of the plaque:
Died for Liberty
on 17 August 1944
at la Metriere
Lougé Sur Maire

20

The Language of the Heart

After the unveiling of the plaque, the ceremony continued. Frederic spoke in French to the assembled group. Roger Bignon stood beside him holding a box. As Frederic finished speaking, eighty-nine year old Roger Pillu attempted to stand. Frederic saw that he was having trouble so he came over to assist him. Finally, he was on his feet. He stood and steadied himself with his cane. He was so distinguished-looking in his gray suit, white hair and neatly groomed, white beard. I wondered if he might be a college professor. The breeze blew gently. A hush fell over the crowd.

Roger Bignon approached with a fabric-covered box. He opened the lid on the box and there it was. I felt myself trembling. This was it.

This is what had brought us to a foreign land over 3,000 miles away from home. This was my connection to my uncle, Jason.

The helmet was handed to Roger Pillu. I'm sure

that the helmet was a sobering reminder of the devastating walk he took many years before. He turned to my father. Dad stood on wobbly legs. He reached out and placed his hands on the helmet. Ryan stood behind Dad to steady him. Both Roger and Dad held the helmet.

Roger Pillu wipes a tear during the speeches.

As tears ran down his cheeks Roger Pillu said:

"In this day of memory, it must be acknowledged that we are all together by the War Memorial, we owe it to Roger Bignon and his friend, René Brideau. They have worked and done everything to find the family of First Lieutenant Jason H. Barron and save him from oblivion, thanks to the

helmet, which I collected on August 17, 1944, close to "la Metriere".

This helmet, stricken by the lethal blow, remained at the disposal of a member of the family who would come to France.

The opportunity thus arose from the 65th anniversary of the Normandy Landings, and six relatives of first Lieutenant Barron are here, one of them being his brother, Mr. Emerson S. Barron.

It is an honor for me to have been indicated to give him, with emotion, the helmet of First Lieutenant Jason H. Barron, this relic which returns to him, to remember the sacrifice of his elder, who died in France at age 23.

I am aware to make him live again for a short time and to think, in this very special day, that he and his five companions, whose names are engraved in stone, are here standing among us today. We cannot forget what we owe to our American friends, and our Allies, and to their thousands of dead during years of war, between 1939 and 1945.

The debt of France towards them is indefeasible.

Honor, honor to you glorious heroes dead for freedom. A Grateful France."

"To Emerson S. Barron, It is with great emotion that I turn back to you the helmet of First Lieutenant Jason H. Barron, your brother, who met death at "la Metriere on August 17, 1944, day of liberation of Lougé-sur-Maire. American friends, you are here welcomed and thank you for attending this memorial ceremony, which marks in an outstanding way the final point "The debt of France towards them is indefeasible. Honor, honor to you glorious heroes dead for freedom. A Grateful France."

After Roger Pillu finished speaking, my father could only make eye contact with Roger Pillu. There were no words. His eyes were glued on the man who cared enough to be the caretaker of this helmet for sixty years. Finally, Dad dropped his head and looked at the helmet and trembled. Having this helmet did not bring his brother back, but receiving it made him understand that the death of the brother he loved was not in vain.

I felt a chill. My eyes glanced around at the people who had come to be part of this solemn occasion. People who had come to see the precious helmet returned to the family they never knew, but had felt a strong connection to for 65 years. This helmet represented that connection. Without it, this day would not have happened. The six soldiers would have been lost to all except fading memories of their families. How would we ever find words to tell these noble men that we would be forever in their debt?

There was no movement for a minute or so.

Roger Pillu, Frederic Blais, and Emerson Barron
Holly looks on tearfully as the helmet is reclaimed.

Quietly, Ryan moved to the microphone to give a short acceptance speech. He had practiced it diligently in French. His voice quivered as he recited it in French.

> *Hello, my name is Ryan Barron. I want to thank you for the opportunity to come here to remember the allied soldiers and people who came*

together to protect France and the World, including my Great Uncle Jason Barron who fought and died with five others in Lougé-sur-Maire.

I was surprised when my aunt told me that my Great Uncle's helmet had been kept safe all this time. I'm grateful to accept it on behalf of my family, including my Grandfather - Jason's brother, who served in the Pacific during the war.

Jason served with the 36th Armored Infantry. I'm told their motto was "Deeds, not Words". I think they lived up to that. Hopefully, we all make them proud. Hopefully, we've proved that our freedom was worth their sacrifice.

Thanks to everyone here, today, and a special thanks to Roger and René for helping us know more about Jason.

"I didn't do a very good job," he said to me after he finished. If only he knew...... he delivered it perfectly.

My father handed the helmet to me. Immediately I noticed the hole. It was an inch in diameter going into the left side. And on the right, the metal around the hole was blown outward. The shrapnel had gone through his brain. Death had come quickly.

Ryan gives his speech of gratitude in French.

21

Lougé-sur-Maire

Mayor Gautier opens the ceremony.

It seems to be a custom of the French people to give a toast on almost any occasion. What a warm and wonderful idea! We huddled in an outdoor shelter while the rain poured. Many stood outside in the rain under umbrellas, but everyone received their champagne. Mayor Marcel Gautier gave a toast.

Now the time came for the lunch to be served.

Over 130 people were seated at round tables with red, white and blue table clothes. At each seat the invitation was perched above the plate. Names were printed on top and they served as our place cards. Someone had gone to a huge amount of effort to make everything so coordinated. The aroma of the food filled the room. The local butcher had prepared the meal. It seemed that all the ladies of the village were knocking themselves out to make us feel comfortable. We were beginning a four hour eating event. As someone who can take two hours to prepare a meal that is consumed in twenty minutes, I was enthralled.

The luncheon had a patriotic theme.

The meal gave us a rest
from the overwhelming events of the day.

Between each course, we were given time to chat with those who were seated nearby. Not being able to engage in conversation, I was content to sit and people-watch. These people cared about each other. They probably had known each other their whole lives. There was so much laughter, so much contentment.

I was sorry that I had not been able to learn some French. I tried to "bone up" on some phrases I had learned many years ago in high school, but they eluded me. I decided a long time ago that learning a foreign language was not my gift. My son speaks four languages fluently including Mandarin Chinese. I can barely handle English.

It was at this gathering that several people came up to us and told us stories that happened during the liberation. I realized that the people in this room had actually lived through the misery of the war.

It was hard for me to understand the reality of war. The closest I had come was on September 11, 2001. I was teaching fourth grade students. Robin, another teacher, came to my door and motioned for me to come out in the hall. She informed me of the horrible events that were unfolding in New York City and at the Pentagon.

I continued to teach, unable to concentrate on the subject. Forty-five minutes later, Robin returned. I was not prepared for what she was about to tell me. The fourth plane had crashed in Shanksville, Somerset County, Pennsylvania. My grandmother Barron had grown up in Shanksville. I had cousins living in Shanksville. As it turned out, the plane crashed less than a mile from where my grandmother had been born. I remember the terror that I felt. I returned to my students and continued by saying, "Tomorrow we will …." I hoped that there would be a tomorrow.

At the luncheon an attractive woman with blonde hair came to me. She had impeccable English. She told me that she had been living in Australia, but had returned for this event. She explained that her father had escaped from Czechoslovakia. He then became a pilot for the French Air Force. One day her father was approaching his airplane to fly on a mission. Someone came running out to him and said, "You needn't go. You have just had a baby girl! Someone else will fly your plane."

The plane was shot down during the mission and the pilot was killed.

This woman before me was that baby girl.

The celebration was larger than we expected. They honored us by clapping three rounds in unison.

After dessert, the mayor went to the podium and spoke to the group. Then Joan and Dad were called to the front of the room. Roger Pillu said a few words and gave gifts to Joan and Dad. One was a glass flask containing soil from the site where Jason and the soldiers died and a small box containing an appreciation card commemorating this event. Dad bravely said a few words of thanks and then Joan took the microphone. In Cajun French she spoke. She cried openly, but she continued until her words of gratitude were finished.

We left the dining hall and were taken to the mayor's office for champagne and gifts.

Among the gifts that we would receive was a black notebook. On the title page is a Swastika on the wall of a building that is covered over by red, white, and blue stripes of paint, expressing the pride and joy of the defeat of the German Occupation. It contains, in the French language, everything about the Argentan-Falaise Gap campaign starting at Pre-Ea-Pail, through Ranes and beyond Fromentel. Photographs show scenes from the war with soldiers, tanks and buildings that escaped the bombing, as well as those that were destroyed. An exposé of the Third Armored Division was featured including an hourly diary of the battle as it unfolded. In addition, it shows the war memorials including today's plaque that honored the valiant efforts of the soldiers.

However, the binder included something truly more precious that gold to me. On nine pages, with drawings of the American and French flags decorating the sides, were messages and signatures of the hundred plus people who attended the ceremony. A few had written their messages in English and their compassion was overwhelming to me.

I was feeling a little bit tired. Little did I know that the evening's events were long from being completed.

22

The Panzer Tank

This is a picture of the actual tank
that provided cover for the six soldiers.

Afterwards we waited outside for the next event. We were told that now we would be taken to the site where the six bodies laid, where they had been covered with an awning and where Roger Pillu had found the helmet. A convoy of cars proceeded down the lane. Soon they started pulling over and parking on the right side in the tall grass. People were exiting their cars, but reverently standing back until my father and Joan approached. My husband, Brian, Hilton, Joan's husband, my nephew, his wife, little Carter, and I followed. We saw the American flag flying above the hedge row. As we got closer we saw the stone marker. The mayor walked up to Dad and Joan with a large bouquet of flowers for them to place before the marker. The sky was azure blue. The clouds were white and fluffy. The grass and trees were so lush and green. Yellow flowers grew nearby, and again, the birds sang.

I turned to Frederic and said, "We passed this way last night?"

"Yes," he said, "we covered it. We didn't want you to know until today."

"This was once an area of massive devastation," he continued as he shook his head.

My brain was searching for answers. Why? Why was this an area of massive devastation? Why were there so many Allied casualties here? What brought them to Lougé-sur-Maire?

Once again it was Frederic who would supply the answers:

> Here is a short military background about events that brought 3rd Armored Division in the area of Lougé:
>
> According to Allied invasion plans, after landing in Normandy on D-Day, Allied armies

were supposed to advance regularly and the German army to successively withdraw under pressure behind rivers and high ground. But what happened did not follow the plans at all. Instead of withdrawing the German fought for every inch. The first phase of the battle of Normandy (from June 6 to July 25) is called the "hedgerows battle" and US Army fought for every village, every farm, every hedgerow and every field. GIs sustained 15% higher casualties than the most pessimistic forecast, especially infantry outfits.

On July 25th Operation Cobra was launched. The German frontline south of Saint-Lô was crushed by massive air bombardment and the 1st Army (General Bradley) opened the way for the 3rd Army (Patton). 3rd Armored Division attacked on the right flank of the 1st Army. A second phase, as unexpected as the first, thus opened in the battle of Normandy.

In the beginning of August, Patton's troops knifed into German lines and strategic points like Avranches or Rennes were sized very easily. Signs were showing that the German Army, after a strong resistance in June and July, was *now totally collapsing. But Allied intelligence had lost the position of four German Armored Divisions (Panzer Division) and they feared these divisions would attack in the Rennes area.*

On August 6th, the German launched their counter-attack, but in Mortain, with Avranches as objective. 3rd AD was in the area of Mortain, they reacted immediately and helped to stop the Germans cold. The failure of German attack gave a great opportunity to Allied generals. Patton was in good position to encircle them. It was then decided that Patton's XV (15th) Corps which was located near le Mans, would attack towards the north and join the British, coming from the area of Caen, to trap German armies in Normandy. They had a "rendez-vous" in Argentan.

The XV Corps attacked alone towards Argentan with opened flanks. The German planned to launch an attack against it, cut it off and destroy it. Four Panzer Divisions were supposed to assemble in the area of Carrouges didn't know anything about German plans, were aware that leaving XV Corps' and then attack towards Alençon on flank opened was too dangerous. 3rd AD was thus sent on the left flank of the XV Corps and ran on August 13th, without knowing it, exactly through the German assembly area. 3rd AD moved fast and initially faced only one Panzer Division, the 1st SS Panzer Division, which was a crack unit. Elements of the remaining Panzer Division (2nd, 9th and 116th) joined the fight later. That's why the battle was so fierce in the area of Rânes-Fromentel, 3rd AD faced alone elements of not less than four Panzer Divisions, but had the job done.

So that is what brought him to beautiful Lougé-sur-Maire and the area known as "Purple Heart Corner."

Roger Bignon prepares to place flowers at the site where the soldiers were attacked on his farm.

I closed my eyes and I envisioned the disabled German Panzer tank sitting in that spot. I saw six brave young soldiers squatting behind it. I heard the gunfire and the approaching German soldiers. I could see and hear the tank working its way toward them. How did they know about the men seeking cover behind the tank, or did they know? I heard the tank fire the round. I saw it hit the trees in the background and explode with a flash of light. I saw the smoke and the shrapnel as it scattered all around. When the smoke cleared, six young soldiers lay lifeless. They had left this life and moved on to something else. They would never know the hugs and kisses and the celebration of returning home. They would never know the warm arms of the woman who would love them. They would never know the feeling of a small child climbing into their lap. They would never again know the comfort of a soft sofa, a good book, a ballgame, or a hearty meal. The life they had been given was over.

Joan and Dad reflect at the site.

23

Ranes

Since we were 330 yards from the Bignon Farm, I assumed we would be going there. I was wrong again.

Everyone got back into their cars and the convoy was on its way again. I wasn't sure where we were going. Brian followed the cars as they turned around and we headed north toward the village. As we passed the church I glanced over at the statue. Yes, the plaque was there. It wasn't a dream.

I asked my dad, "How are you doing?"

"I'm glad I came," he replied.

It was very comforting to hear this. He looked weary, but he looked as though a load of grief had been lifted off his shoulders.

Before we had left Maryland, I thought to myself, "Am I putting too much on an eighty-three year old man?" I had even said to my sister jokingly, "Will you get angry with me if Daddy dies over there? Am I killing him?"

"No, the final decision will be his. He needs to be there. Just so he's happy," my sister answered with a grin.

I wish my sister and brother could have been there. My sister, Nancy, is a teacher and could not get away in May. My brother, Randy, was tied up in business that made it impossible for him to get away.

We lost our younger brother, Scott, three years earlier, at the age of 48, due to a massive heart attack. Ryan is his son.

It was very special to me that Ryan and his young family were able to be part of this occasion. After his father died, Ryan had accepted a job offer and moved to Delaware. I was afraid we would see him less and less often and eventually lose contact.

I know how hard it is to lose a brother. Now Dad had also lost a child.

We proceeded six miles until we came to the town of Ranes. The cars pulled into the parking lot of the town hall. It was a large stone building with a very tall watch tower. It looked somewhat like a castle. We were told that this building had served as the S.S. headquarters for three days while the Germans occupied the town.

The town hall was used as the headquarters for the S.S. for three days.

We climbed the 95 steps. I counted. We came out to an open area at the top of the tower. About thirty of us had ascended the stairs. You could see the whole town and the orange terra cotta roofs. The narrow streets wound through the stone buildings. All was quiet in the village. The view was majestic.

Frederic opened his binder of maps and showed us how the battle had moved through Normandy. He pointed out across the fields and showed us how the troops proceeded inland. The red arrows show the directions of attack. Each page of maps was marked, D+22 (D-Day plus 22 days), D+38, D+44, then he came to D+72 - August 17, 1944, three years and one day before

I was born.

He explained that Company F was headed to Fromentel, but in order to cover the flank, troops were sent to the east. My uncle and his men were sent to Lougé-sur-Maire, where they were met with heavy artillery. I had just received a lesson in World War II history.

Gathering on the tower for a history lesson.

We descended the steps and went into a beautiful room called the wedding room. There we were shown a black and white movie of actual events that had taken place in Ranes during the occupation. We also heard the story about five American soldiers who were taken prisoner on the first day. One understood German and he overheard them say that they would be executed that night. The Americans began their assault with a heavy bombing barrage. The men used the loud noise and the commotion as an opportunity to escape. Two made it to freedom. Three were caught in the field and were shot in the back of the head on the spot.

I walked through the small town. I admired the lovely stone buildings and the cobblestone streets. There were no convenience stores or gas stations. I could see the flat, green, rolling meadows that surrounded the town. It was probably very similar to the way it was in 1944.

A view of Ranes from the tower.

24
Reflection of the Day

We went back to the Bignon Farm for dinner. There was a lot of chatter and laughter. Everyone was pleased with the success of the day. All the hard work in bringing this together had paid off. Dad was exhausted and quiet. He was asked several times if he was okay. He was enjoying all the attention. Again the ladies prepared a delicious meal. We were served Roger's delicious homemade sweet apple cider. Joan asked how he made it taste so good. The apples of the area gave it its special flavor. He told us that this was given to the American soldiers by the farmers.

The folks sang French songs to us. Brian sang "La Bamba" and the group joined in on the chorus. We also enjoyed Roger's homemade wine. I will never enjoy wine again as much as I did that night at the Bignon farm in Lougé-sur-Maire, France.

Frederic now had an opportunity to show us his book on helmets. He, along with Regis Giard, had researched and published a large book on helmets titled, Helmets of the ETO (Europe Theatre of Operations), A Historical and Technical Guide. Jason's helmet was one of a few that could be positively identified.

The book was impressive. It was a large book. It contained an enormous amount of information about helmets. It also contained pictures of helmets that had been gathered after the war. His research took him to museums and private collections.

Two of the many gifts that we received:
a book from a new friend and
Jason's helmet.

Frederic gave us signed copies of his book, and asked each of us to sign his copy. He would keep it as a reminder of this special occasion. It had been published in English and in French. Frederic had grown up near Lougé-sur-Maire. He had an insatiable thirst to learn all he could about WWII.

He was in his early thirties, very handsome and very well-spoken. His English was very good. But what struck me most was his compassion. Throughout the day, we had seen it many times in his eyes and heard it in his voice. He had played a huge part in making this celebration happen.

He gave a book to Ryan, to my father, and to me. He had already sent one to my aunt in Jacksonville, Florida. She had given him permission to include Jason's helmet in the book.

He wrote the following inscriptions in English in my book:

To Linda and Brian,
I will never forget this very special day
and the feeling to meet real friends.
See you again in the U.S. maybe.

Friendly,
F. Blais
Lougé-sur-Maire
05-23-09

In my father's book he wrote:

To Mr. Emerson Barron,
It is a great emotion to sign this book which is a
tribute to WWII veterans and especially soldiers
who answered the call of their country and paid
the ultimate price, what was the most precious,
their life.

> *A grateful French,*
> *F. Blais*
> *Lougé-sur-Maire*
> *05/23/09*

Jason's helmet is featured in Frederic's book.

Again I gazed around the room. I watched as, Genevieve, Gigi, and Marie Antoinette threw back their heads in laughter as Joan related a story in Cajun French. I watched Ryan and Frederic deep in conversation at the other end of the table. I marveled at Roger as he continued to be the perfect host and make sure everyone's glass was filled with wine. I chuckled at René and his booming laughter. Every person in the room was involved in conversation. No one was left out. Friendships were being forged - friendships that were destined to last a lifetime.

Everyone gathers for a final picture
to commemorate our time together

25

Gorron

The following morning we awoke at the quaint Bed and Breakfast where we were staying. We went down to the dining room for breakfast.

The chef gave us a big smile and came out from around the breakfast bar nodding his head and pointing to the newspaper he had in his hand. It had an article about the ceremony. Dad, Joan, and the mayor were pictured on the front page. There was a big article with the picture. I could not read the French, but I knew what it said.

After breakfast, Frederic and René came to lead us to the town of Gorron. I asked Frederic what was going to happen there. He said it would be very special. We drove about a half an hour into a larger village. The countryside was quaint. We didn't see modern buildings, stores or construction. We passed an occasional car.

We met up with a group of cars at the town hall and were immediately motioned to turn around and follow the succession of cars. Turning was tight, but we were soon on our way. We traveled a short distance out of town. We were out in the country in a very open, flat, area. There were lots of fields that were being prepared for the planting of crops.

Gorron was the temporary cemetery for soldiers during WW II.

As we approached, I saw about a hundred cars parked in the field on the right. We were quite surprised to see many dignitaries. Mayor Jean-Marc Allain was pointed out to us. He was wearing a sash that hung to his waist with a large bronze medallion. He was very handsome and had a strong jaw. Several mayors from nearby villages and towns were introduced.

We soon learned that this was the temporary

cemetery for 752 soldiers. Included in that number were the bodies of Jason Barron, Levy Guidry, Jessie C. Price, Michael Koepl, Arthur A. Hudson, and David Williams.

Jason's temporary grave at Gorron.

They had been buried here until they would be sent for permanent burial either at home or in France on land that was set aside for British and American soldiers. It was a flat field, several acres in size. Rows of tiny green plants were peeking through the soil.

I wondered how this event had come about. Later I learned that Frederic had gone to Gorron for information. When the people of Gorron heard that the American families were coming to reclaim the helmet and join in the dedication of the plaque at Lougé-sur-Maire, they wanted to honor the Americans also.

Levy's temporary grave at Gorron

We got out of the car and walked down the lane with the people. We arrived at a place where about a dozen chairs had been set up facing a monument draped with the American flag. The French flag and the American flags flanked whatever it was that was being hidden. As always, there was a huge arrangement of flowers in front of the draped flag. We were motioned to take a seat. Several other folks who were most likely in their eighties also sat on the chairs that had been provided.

A succession of people spoke briefly. There was a local language teacher translating in very broken English. We were given English copies of the speeches. I didn't follow along. I was intrigued with the passion in the faces of the speakers. Frederic rose to go to the microphone.

Many shared their stories and grief.

As he spoke I could see his emotions had gotten the best of him. He struggled to fight back tears and to keep his voice from trembling. This young man had so thoroughly researched the atrocities of this era that it was almost as if he had lived through the events himself.

There were many uniformed people: military, police, and firemen. A public address system was set up. Here is one of the speeches that we would read later that would help us understand how this ceremony had come about:

> *Ladies and gentlemen and dear friends, We are together today, on May 24, 2009, to pay homage to the 752 American soldiers whose provisional burial took place in this field during the period of*

GUERRE
1939 - 1945

En mémoire de
l'inhumation provisoire
des 752 soldats américains
de 1944 à 1948

Levy and Jason represent all of those that were buried here.

1944 to 1948.

During that period, the people from Gorron and from the surrounding area often came to meditate and to place flowers on the tombs of their liberators, walking from Gorron, behind the American military band and behind the band of the town. I am going to read the speech which was made by the American officer who was responsible for the ceremony at the cemetery on November 11, 1944. After the relocation of the bodies in 1948, either to St. James or to the States, the ceremony took place on May 8 in Gorron beside the monument to the dead.

Let us tell a little about this period. I wasn't in Gorron at that time. I lived at my parent's house, not far from Mortain. It reminds me of the eight days during which bullets made holes in the roof of the house, so we had to sleep in a quarry. Because the German Red Cross was established in the town hall in Gorron, our town wasn't bombed after the D-Day Invasion on June 6, 1944. However, there were a lot of casualties around Mortain and in the next department called Orne, ending at Mont Ormel at the end of August 1944. Very quickly the Germans suffered large casualties.

After burying a hundred bodies next to the cemetery of the town, they had to choose another field to bury more that 2200 dead soldiers. The first American Soldier died on August 4, 1944.

In September 2008, I had a call from Mr. Frederic Blais who asked me about the American cemetery in Gorron and about the possibility of a visit for the American families.

I informed Mr. Jean-Marc Allain, Mayor of Gorron, who told me about a project. The town council wanted to place a stele to immortalize this place in memory of our American soldiers.

Yesterday, a first ceremony took place in Lougé-sur-Maire where some American soldiers were killed. Today the American families who are with us are going to unveil the stele in honour of the 752 dead soldiers who fought to preserve our freedom.

To finish, I want to tell you that two men wrote to keep alive the memory of the difficult period of our area. They are Mr. Michel Bechet and Mr. Maxime Poirier.

The folowing speech was given by an American Officer on Veteran's Day in 1944:

To our very dear French friends of Gorron and of the area:

It is on Saturday, November 11, 1944, in the American Cemetery in Gorron that the true feelings of French people were revealed to us.

In spite of the bad weather, a lot of people paid homage to our friends in this cemetery. You can believe me if I say that when we write to our families or when we go back to America, we will transmit to our families and to the families who have lost a father, or son, or a husband, all the affection you showed during those two days, in honor of our absent friends.

We hope that next year at the same time, peace will be signed and that the Americans among our group who will still be alive, will return to the States with the great consolation to know that all those we left behind, will always be honored by you.

The words of November 11, 1944, turned out to be true. The French people of Normandy continued to honor the soldiers, living and dead, who sacrificed for their freedom.

Next an elderly man with a cane was helped to the microphone. He looked out over the crowd. He tried to speak, but sorrow overcame him. He had been the caretaker of the cemetery. As he told the story he openly cried and struggled to continue with his voice rising and falling. This man was assigned the duty of taking care of the bodies of the 752 soldiers. These soldiers had died to give him freedom - to give his family freedom.

He was serious and conscientious about the task that was laid before him. Each body received the utmost respect and dignity. He marked each plot so that the soldiers would not be lost to infamy. He treated each body as though it were his brother. This man lived with what he had seen every day of his life. My father looked straight ahead at the field as the man continued. Someone had cared about his brother's lifeless body. Again, I saw a look of peace in my father's eyes.

The flag was pulled away by Joan and Dad. The sacred monument was unveiled. This would be hallowed ground forever.

A recording of The Star Spangled Banner was played. The Americans covered their hearts with their hands. The French stood at attention.

Next, a recording of the French National Anthem was played, but it stopped. They started the recording again, but again it stopped. The mayor said something, the crowd laughed, and then people started to mingle.

A small, youthful-looking lady came up to me and spoke to me in French. She so much wanted me to understand the story she was trying to relate. I nodded my head and smiled as though I did understand. I moved on to the next person who was waiting to share their story.

Another woman came up to Holly and pointed across the field on the other side of the road. She said an American airplane had landed there.

The ceremony prepares to move into the town hall.

A young man in his twenties came to my father. He had pictures of a Republic B-47 Thunderbird airplane. It was important to him that Dad was able to see the pictures. Dad took his time and studied the pictures. He returned them to the young man and shook his hand in gratitude. This act was so appreciated by my father. Dad, having been in the Army Air Force, had a great interest in war airplanes.

Several people walked up to us. They wanted to tell us stories. Some were translated into English for us. It kept the French people who were able to speak English very busy.

An elderly man came up to us with tears running down his face. As he spoke, Frederic translated. The Germans took his town over for one day. He was taken prisoner. He was told that he would be executed as soon as some other business was finished. On that day the Americans came. The man was traded for two German prisoners. Is it any wonder that these people felt so much gratitude toward us, the families of the brave soldiers?

Another lady came to Holly and said that she had moved to France many years ago. Her neighbor had a farm. They were putting a new roof on the barn when a bomb was discovered in the rafters. The military came and put red tape around the area.   A team came to disarm the bomb. The scary part was that her children and grandchildren played in the barn.

On the road again, we headed back to Gorron. We were led into the town hall and up the stairs to a large community room. Dad went to the bathroom and someone came to try to hurry him along, but you can't hurry Dad went he is in the bathroom.

Finally Dad came out. We walked into the room. There was a standing ovation. We were handed a glass of champagne and toasted by the mayor.

Several people spoke. Dad surprised us by standing up and walking to the podium. I expected him to choke up, but in complete control he spoke from his heart:

Mayor Jean-Marc Allain leads everyone in a toast.

"Greetings to all the many new friends and dignitaries who are attending this celebration. I did not come prepared for a speech. I will say very few words. I believe I can speak from my heart, (at this point, his voice broke) the gratitude of myself, my family, and the remembrance of my brother. For 65 years, I did not know the circumstances of my brother's death. I didn't know if his name would be forgotten in the annals of history.

When I return with my family to the United States, I will be one of the best ambassadors France could ever have in the United States. This is an *experience I did not expect. But believe me, I am overwhelmed with the greatness and the friendship the French people have shown to us.*

In the sixty-five years since the death of my brother, Jason, I would have many dreams about him... and I would always be awakened... and I'd be crying. When I go home I will not need to cry...any more. I know that the love and affection that you have shown my family and me since we have been here is more emotional and heartfelt than anything else you could have done for me.

So as I part from you I will go home, I will remember you, and the best I can say is thank you from the bottom of my heart."

Later, we asked him if it was hard to speak with the lady interrupting him to translate. "No," he said. "That gave me time to think about what I was going to say next."

I was very proud of him.

They tried to play La Marseillaise, their national anthem again, and again the recording failed. At that, the people began to sing their anthem with pride. They sang out loud and strong and the tears streamed down my face. Here is the English translation:

Let's go children of the fatherland,
The day of glory has arrived!

Against us tyranny's
Bloody flag is raised! (repeat)
In the countryside, do you hear
The roaring of these fierce soldiers?
They come right to our arms
To slit the throats of our sons, our friends!
Let's go children of the fatherland,
The day of glory has arrived!
Against us tyranny's
Bloody flag is raised! (repeat)
In the countryside, do you hear
The roaring of these fierce soldiers?
They come right to our arms
To slit the throats of our sons, our friends!

Refrain

Grab your weapons, citizens!
Form your batallions!
Let us march! Let us march!
May impure blood
Water our fields!

This horde of slaves, traitors, plotting kings,
What do they want?
For whom these vile shackles,
These long-prepared irons? (repeat)

Frenchmen, for us, oh! what an insult!
What emotions that must excite!
It is us that they dare to consider
Returning to ancient slavery!

What! These foreign troops
Would make laws in our home!
What! These mercenary phalanxes
Would bring down our proud warriors! (repeat)
Good Lord! By chained hands
Our brows would bend beneath the yoke!
Vile despots would become
The masters of our fate!

Tremble, tyrants! and you, traitors,
The disgrace of all groups,
Tremble! Your parricidal plans
Will finally pay the price! (repeat)
Everyone is a soldier to fight you,
If they fall, our young heroes,
France will make more,
Ready to battle you!

Refrain

Sacred love of France,
Lead, support our avenging arms!

Liberty, beloved Liberty,
Fight with your defenders! (repeat)
Under our flags, let victory
Hasten to your manly tones!
May your dying enemies
See your triumph and our glory!

We will enter the pit
When our elders are no longer there;
There, we will find their dust
And the traces of their virtues. (repeat)
Much less eager to outlive them
Than to share their casket,
We will have the sublime pride
Of avenging them or following them!

La Marseillaise was composed by Claude-Joseph Rouget de Lisle in 1792 and was declared the French national anthem in 1795.

The hospitality of these wonderful people continued. Twenty-five guests joined the mayor at a local restaurant where we were served cocktails, puffy pastries and wine, scallops and baby vegetables, a choice of beef or quail, and a decadent chocolate dessert. After dessert, the group continued to talk. Carter had been sitting a long time and was getting restless. I used this as an excuse

We gathered for pictures in the community room of the town hall.

to leave the table. I needed a minute to compose myself. It was soon going to be over. I would never again see these people whom I had grown to cherish. This weekend had truly been a wonderful tribute to all soldiers of all nations who have given their lives in the name of freedom.

There was a playground behind the restaurant, and Carter and I walked out to a swing set. I pushed him on the swing a little while and then he got off and sat on the ladder on the side swinging his leg and kicking a chain. He said to me, "There's a boy named Scott in my house. He has a ball. Sometimes he plays ball with me. One time I fell and he said, "Did you hurt yourself?"

Holly walked up as he said this. She shook her head. Later she told me, "No. He doesn't have a friend named Scott."

On the day that he died, my brother, Scott, did something unusual. He went home for lunch and played with Carter, his one-year-old grandson whom he dearly loved. I still experience the stunned feeling that came over me when Carter told me this story. Perhaps it was an imaginary playmate. But, I believe that Scott had truly visited him, just as I believe that Jason, Levy, Arthur, Michael, Jessie, and David were present when the people of Lougé-sur-Maire and Gorron honored them for their sacrifice.

It was soon time to say our good-byes. We invited everyone to be our guests in America. That would be an unimaginable pleasure. I turned to say good-bye to René. For two years we had conversed via email with the computer translating our messages. While in France I hardly spoke to him. After hugging him, I made a type-writing gesture with my fingers. When I got back to the United States, I would be better able to communicate with him through emails and the "imperfect" translations.

26

Farewell to Normandy

After the weekend, we drove to Paris and did some sightseeing on Monday. Ryan, Holly, Carter and Dad would be flying home in the morning. Brian and I were going to stay a few more days and travel on to Brugge, Belgium. Brian and I decided to take the shuttle to the airport to find out if there would be any problem transporting the helmet home. The agent called the main office for clarification. We were assured that we could pack it in our large suitcase and it would be alright. After sixty-five years of waiting, we certainly did not want to lose the helmet now. While we were there, we decided to upgrade Dad's seat to business class.

Some interesting things happened while we were in Paris. They are unrelated to this story but somehow they seem to fit.

We had gone to a McDonald's to eat. We were dying for a coke with some ice. That was our only complaint in Europe. Very little ice is put in drinks. As a matter of fact, on our return flight, Brian would say to the flight attendant, "If I ask for more ice in my drink would I be irritating?"

"No, "she grinned, "You would be American."

At McDonald's a very sharp-looking, clean-cut young man sat at a table near us.

Upon hearing our American voices, he asked in a deep southern drawl, "Where are you from?"

"We are from Maryland," was my reply, "How about you?"

"Ma'am, I am from Alabama. We are in the United States Marine Corp. We are here in France to be part of the Memorial Day Celebrations," the Marine said respectfully.

Two more Marines joined him at his table. One was from Virginia, and the other was from Missouri. At that, my father asked if he could sit with them. He told them why we were in France and about his own experience in the military. When the Marine asked him what he did in the Army Air Force, my father replied, "We cleaned up after the Marines."

That brought a laugh from all of us. Then something very special happened. The Marine from Alabama gave my father a medallion that had been passed down through his family. It had the Marine Corps symbol on one side and the Mason symbol on the other. He had noticed Dad's ring.

I wish I could find these young men and tell them how very much this act of kindness and respect meant to an eighty-three year old veteran.

When we arrived back in Maryland, I went to Dad's home to see if he had recovered from the trip. He was very happy. He said he certainly did enjoy the upgrade on the flight home, but something had happened that he was embarrassed about, and it was keeping him awake at nights. He said the flight attendants were taking very good care of him. He had all he wanted to eat and drink. However, they brought him a newspaper. He opened it and there on the front page was a picture that caused him to lose control of his emotions. He cried and shook and he couldn't make himself stop. The flight attendants all came to him and were very concerned. It took quite a while before he had enough composure to explain to them why the newspaper had upset him.

A picture of a flag-draped coffin was on the front page of the newspaper.

27

Getting to Know "J.C."

PFC Jessie C. Price
Born in 1921
Age at death: 23
Wilbarger, Texas
KIA: August 17, 1944
Lougé-sur-Maire

Since I have arrived home, it seems that my binder has continued to grow exponentially.

There was a stack of mail waiting for me. I saw the envelope that I wanted to open first. Jessie's sister, Marjorie, and his niece, Inez, had made pictures of J.C. for me. I sat down on my sofa and studied his face. He was the picture of innocence. Now I could give Jessie the space he deserved in my binder.

They also sent some official documents and a brief history of his family. Jessie was one of eight children. He was fifteen when his mother died of a kidney ailment.

J.C.'s sister, Marjorie, with deceased husband, Leon.

I talked with his sister, Marjorie, again to tell her about the ceremonies. Eighty-three years of age and she still takes care of her family. I hope someday to drive to Texas and meet this wonderful lady and her daughter.

Like so many families during the war, the fire of their grief would be kindled by the telegrams and letters that would announce, and then remind them that Jessie was gone. The only hope they would have is that his body would be brought home to them.

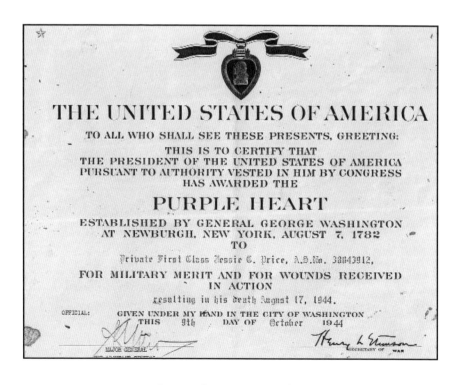

J.C.'s Purple Heart certificate.

WAR DEPARTMENT

THE ADJUTANT GENERAL'S OFFICE

WASHINGTON 25, D. C.

8 September 1944

Mr. Monroe F. Price
Route Number One, Box 31
Vernon, Texas

Dear Mr. Price:

It is with regret that I am writing to confirm the recent telegram informing you of the death of your brother, Private First Class Jessie C. Price, 38,043,912, Infantry, who was killed in action on 17 August 1944 in France.

I fully understand your desire to learn as much as possible regarding the circumstances leading to his death and I wish that there were more information available to give you. Unfortunately, reports of this nature contain only the briefest details as they are prepared under battle conditions and the means of transmission are limited.

I know the sorrow this message has brought you and it is my hope that in time the knowledge of his heroic service to his country, even unto death, may be of sustaining comfort to you.

I extend to you my deepest sympathy.

Sincerely yours,

J. A. ULIO
Major General,
The Adjutant General.

1 Inclosure
· Bulletin of Information.

Letter from the War Department confirming J.C. was K.I.A.

In GRATEFUL MEMORY OF

Private First Class Jessie G. Price, A.S.No. 38043912,

WHO DIED IN THE SERVICE OF HIS COUNTRY AT

in the European Area, August 17, 1944.

STANDS IN THE UNBROKEN LINE OF PATRIOTS /WHO HAVE DARED TO DIE

THAT FREEDOM MIGHT LIVE, AND GROW, AND INCREASE ITS BLESSINGS.

FREEDOM LIVES, AND THROUGH IT, HE LIVES—

IN A WAY THAT HUMBLES THE UNDERTAKINGS OF MOST MEN

Franklin D Roosevelt

Condolences and Thanks from President Roosevelt.

28
Michael and the Patriot

PFC Michael E. Koepl
Born: 1913
Age at Death: 31
Chippewa Falls, Wisconsin
KIA: August 17, 1944
Lougé-sur-Maire

Among the treasures in my mailbox, there was a package from Edward J. Nayes. He sent me pictures of Michael Koepl, his gravestone, and a picture of the small cemetery where he is buried. The infamous date of August 17, 1944 stands out.

Wilson Cemetery where Michael
and some of his family members are buried.

Ed sent me a list of the names of sisters and brothers. They are all deceased. However, Michael had nieces and nephews living in Wisconsin. Ed was persistent in his search to find the family of Michael Koepl. I received a list of names and addresses of eleven nieces and nephews. I wrote to all of them and sent a picture of the plaque in Lougé-sur-Maire. Two nieces contacted me - Carol Meyers and Jeanette Geist. Jeanette related a story to me. She said that right before he left for Europe, Michael told his mother, "If I don't find the medal I lost, I won't be coming home."

Jeanette said she wasn't sure what the medal was, but he did not find it.

This is the first picture
of Michael's gravestone that I received.

At the next family gathering they are going to spend time speaking with other members of the family to learn more about their uncle who died 65 years ago. They will pass the information they gather on to me. I hope this will give them more knowledge of their family history as it did for me.

In a recent email, Carol told me that the new information about her uncle has encouraged her children to learn more about Michael and World War II.

My dad's goal is being accomplished - that young people would be more aware of the cost of freedom.

In addition, she said that she has a cousin living in St. Louis. He remembers the big fire that destroyed the army archives in 1973.

There was a sad note in this story. Michael's mother died between the time she received the telegram of regrets and the time Michael's body arrived in America.

The story about Michael being honored in France has generated interest in the cemetery where he is buried. Ed restored his headstone.

Through newspaper articles, I learned much more about the work Ed is doing. Ed is the founder of an organization that puts on military tributes. He has refurbished many memorials and dedicated many plaques so that these brave soldiers will not be forgotten. Recently, he learned that a friend of his mother had a brother who was MIA. He lamented over the fact that there had never been a service to honor his brother. Ed went into action and arranged to have a funeral service with honors for all MIAs of 1942. Ed also saw to it that a plaque was ordered and put in the local cemetery.

Ed has also created a fund so that this work can continue so future generations will be aware of these events in our history.

Here is the stone after it was cleaned.

Ed's organization that honors the memories of lost soldiers.

In his next call, he told me that he had just returned from helping with a military funeral of a soldier who had died in Iraq.

Thanks to Ed, the day came when I could tell Michael's nephews and nieces about the hero in their ancestry and show them the pictures of the memorials in France that honor their uncle. To me, Edward J. Nayes is also Michael's family.

Ed did something that pleased me immensely. On May 23, 2009, he published an outstanding article in the local newspaper in Wisconsin about what was happening in France on that day. Now the people would know about the young man from their community. This was important to me.

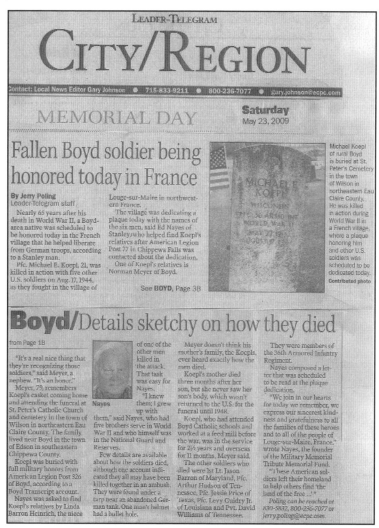

LEADER-TELEGRAM

CITY/REGION

Contact: Local News Editor Gary Johnson ● 715-833-9211 ● 800-236-7077 ● gary.johnson@ecpc.com

MEMORIAL DAY

Saturday
May 23, 2009

Fallen Boyd soldier being honored today in France

By Jerry Poling
Leader-Telegram staff

Nearly 65 years after his death in World War II, a Boyd-area native was scheduled to be honored today in the French village that he helped liberate from German troops, according to a Stanley man.

Pfc. Michael E. Koepl, 21, was killed in action with five other U.S. soldiers on Aug. 17, 1944, as they fought in the village of

Louge-sur-Maire in northwestern France.

The village was dedicating a plaque today with the names of the six men, said Ed Nayes of Stanley, who helped find Koepl's relatives after American Legion Post 77 in Chippewa Falls was contacted about the dedication.

One of Koepl's relatives is Norman Meyer of Boyd.

See BOYD, Page 3B

Michael Koepl of rural Boyd is buried at St. Peter's Cemetery in the town of Wilson in northeastern Eau Claire County. He was killed in action during World War II in a French village, where a plaque honoring him and other U.S. soldiers was scheduled to be dedicated today.
Contributed photo

Boyd/Details sketchy on how they died

from Page 1B

"It's a real nice thing that they're recognizing those soldiers," said Meyer, a nephew. "It's an honor."

Meyer, 79, remembers Koepl's casket coming home and attending the funeral at St. Peter's Catholic Church and cemetery in the town of Wilson in northeastern Eau Claire County. The family lived near Boyd in the town of Edson in southeastern Chippewa County.

Koepl was buried with full military honors from American Legion Post 326 of Boyd, according to a Boyd Transcript account.

Nayes was asked to find Koepl's relatives by Linda Barron Heinrich, the niece

of one of the other men killed in the attack. That task was easy for Nayes.

"I knew them; I grew up with them," said Nayes, who had five brothers serve in World War II and who himself was in the National Guard and Reserves.

Few details are available about how the soldiers died, although one account indicated they all may have been killed together in an ambush. They were found under a tarp near an abandoned German tank. One man's helmet had a bullet hole.

Nayes

Mayer doesn't think his mother's family, the Koepls, ever heard exactly how the men died.

Koepl's mother died three months after her son, but she never saw her son's body, which wasn't returned to the U.S. for the funeral until 1948.

Koepl, who had attended Boyd Catholic schools and worked at a feed mill before the war, was in the service for 2½ years and overseas for 11 months, Meyer said.

The other soldiers who died were 1st Lt. Jason Barron of Maryland, Pfc. Arthur Hudson of Tennessee, Pfc. Jessie Price of Texas, Pfc. Levy Guidry Jr. of Louisiana and Pvt. David Williams of Tennessee.

They were members of the 36th Armored Infantry Regiment.

Nayes composed a letter that was scheduled to be read at the plaque dedication.

"We join in our hearts for today we remember, we express our sincerest kindness and gratefulness to all the families of these heroes and to all of the people of Louge-sur-Maire, France," wrote Nayes, the founder of the Military Memorial Tribute Memorial Fund.

"These American soldiers left their homeland to help others find 'the land of the free ...'"

Poling can be reached at 830-5832, 800-236-7077 or jerry.poling@ecpc.com.

The article that Ed put in the paper to coincide with the memorial service in France.

The headline on 1B from the newspaper article stated that the details were sketchy on how the soldiers died. The article had not made a mistake. We learned

223

so much about that sad day and we would need to set the record straight.

> ## Remembering Their Sacrifice
> ### In Tribute of Remembering Love
>
> I personally, feel the honors of the people of Louge Sur Maire, France to Stand-forth and recognize the past WWII American Heroes: 1st Lt. Jason H. Barron, PFC. Arthur A. Hudson, PFC. Jessie C. Price, PFC Levy A. Guidry Jr., PVT. David M. Williams, PFC. Michael E. Koepl.
>
> These American Soldiers, left their homeland to the Battlefields of War to Preserve their Country and to help others to find "The land of the free and the home of the brave."
>
> I/we the people always remember the bravery of the men and women who has given the reflections of light with solemn pride in the heroism of those who died for our country in service with gratitude that others may live for our freedom, liberty, justice for all.
>
> On this 23rd day of May 2009, the people of Louge sur maire, France along with the family of 1st Lt. Jason H. Barron in commemoration to all these American Heroes, today as the people of Louge sur maire, France are all together in celebration of love in dedication to our American Fallen Heroes for their willingness to serve.
>
> I/we join in our hearts for today we remember, we express our sincerest kindness and greatfulness to all the families of these heroes and to of all the people of Louge sur maire, France.
>
> Thank you for your respectfulness to our American Heroes. Love you all! "May we always remember the love." As script;
>
> Military Memorial Tribute
> Memorial Fund
> c/o Edward J. Nayes
> 108 W 9th Ave. #5
> Stanley, WJ 54768

A letter from Ed to the people of Normandy.

I will be forever grateful to Edward J. Nayes for the work he does to honor all American Veterans, prisoners of war, those who are missing in action, and those who have been killed in action.

Ed is helping me to get a memorial that will be placed in front of my grandfather and grandmother's gravestone at St. John's Cemetery in Somerset, Pennsylvania. It will signify that their son, First Lieutenant Jason H. Barron, who died in service to his country, is buried in Brittany American Cemetery in St. James, France.

29
Adell and the Anonymous Gift

PFC Arthur A. Hudson
Born: 1923
Age at Death: 21
Lawrenceburg, Tennessee
KIA: August 17, 1944
Lougé-sur-Maire

The biggest surprise came when I opened my emails and received a message from Janet Heim. She was the reporter who wrote the article about the helmet for our local newspaper. She had received an email from Deborah Miles from Bowling Green, Kentucky. Someone had sent her a copy of the article. She was asking Janet for information about the people mentioned in the article. Deborah Miles wanted desperately to locate the family of First Lieutenant Jason H. Barron. She was the cousin of Arthur A. Hudson, who was known by his middle name, Adell.

Deborah and I spoke on the phone. It was so wonderful to hear how interested she was in the fate of her cousin. She had been doing a search of her family ancestry.

It is quite a mystery, but an Englishman who had a summer home near Lougé-sur-Maire had seen her name on ancestry.com and sent her the article from our local newspaper. To this day, I do not know if the man was at the ceremony.

Anyway, wherever he is, I want him to know, we are very grateful for this anonymous gift. Thanks to him, we made contact with the final family. My mission was accomplished.

I am also grateful to the reporter, Janet Heim, for her interest in the story, and including the information and details that enabled us to find the family of Arthur

Adell Hudson.

Deborah had very little information about Adell and did not have any pictures of him. However, she sent me the obituary of Adell's sister, Estelle Methvin. It stated that she had three daughters and listed the towns where they lived. I found the address of two of the daughters on the internet. I got busy and wrote to each of the sisters. I didn't know what to expect. It had been so many years. Did all of this matter to them?

Just as the other families had responded to hearing about their loved one, so it was with the Hudson/ Methvin family. I sent my letter on Friday and, by Sunday, I heard from sisters, Norma Ruhling and Linda Smith. I also received a call from Jana White, the daughter of the third sister, Dee Myhan.

Linda made me promise to send pictures of the plaque to her as soon as I hung up the phone. She wouldn't allow me to hang up until she was satisfied that I was sending the picture immediately. She was so anxious to see the plaque. Later, I heard from her. Her email was very emotional. She is now hoping that she will be able to go to Lougé-sur-Maire and the Normandy Coast so she can see the plaque in person and meet the people who care so much.

Linda Smith scanned several items and sent them to me. She sent a small picture of Adell, along with a picture of the flag that draped his casket and his

Purple Heart medal in a frame. She also sent a note that he had written to Estelle with part of the inscription blacked-out.

She told me that Adell's great-grandmother was a full-blooded Cherokee Indian who had marched in the Trail of Tears.

She also remembered the day her mother received the news that her brother had been killed in France. Linda was six years-old. A man came to he door. He talked to her mother and she collapsed into a chair. Linda couldn't understand, but she knew something awful had happened.

As Linda and I spoke on the phone, I could tell that the memories were returning to her vividly. Slowly and softly she spoke. She remembers that when she was around nine years-of-age, the casket came home. They were allowed to open the casket. Inside the casket there was a small bag that contained a piece of the uniform, two dog tags, and a lighter. These memories were so clear to her now.

Unfortunately, it is believed that Adell received a "Dear John" letter shortly before his death.

Jana, Adell's great-niece, had a nice picture of Adell made and sent to me.

Here is the V-Mail that Adell sent to his sister:

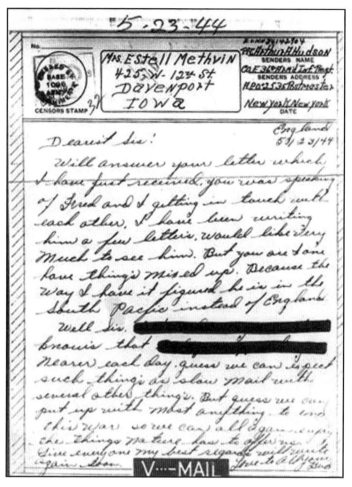

Adell's V-mail to his sister.

It reads as follows:

England
5/23/44

Dearest Sis:

Will answer your letter which I have just received. You were speaking of Fred and I getting in touch with each other. I have been writing him a few letters. Would like very much to see him. But you or I have things messed up. Because the way I have it figured he is in the South Pacific instead of England.

Well Sis ███████████████████████████ ████████████████ nearer each day. Guess we can expect such things as slow mail with several things. But guess we can put up with most anything to end this war. So we can all again (accept) the things that nature has to offer us. Give everyone my best regards. Will write again soon.

Love, your brother.

Arthur's final resting place.

Linda Smith helped me get the forms to replace the Purple Heart certificates that had been misplaced. The certificates are needed for the display at the Purple Heart Museum in New York. They plan to display the pictures and certificates of the six soldiers together. She told me that she got the information to order Adell's certificate from her grandmother's Bible. This reminded me of how important it is to keep good records of our family history.

My dream had come to fruition. I had a picture to put with the name of each soldier. I had made the families aware of the honor that was being bestowed on the soldiers in Lougé-sur-Maire and Gorron, France. I had learned about each of them through the stories that were shared with me. The circle of the families of the soldiers who had taken cover behind the disabled Panzer tank on August 17, 1944 was complete.

Adell's Purple Heart

234

30

The Unfortunate Reality

One morning my husband and I were sitting on the porch talking about the trip to Lougé-sur-Maire. We pulled out a folder that was given to us in Gorron. It seemed to be information that was shared at a previous celebration. We have not translated it, but it appears to be the activities that took place around Gorron, Brece, and Mayenne. The pictures were all very interesting, showing planes, bulldozers, minesweepers, an emergency airstrip and, of course, the temporary burial grounds. There was one paper of some length in English. We spent some time reading it.

The title of it was Graves Registration During World War II in Europe 603 Quartermaster Graves Registration Company by LTC (then SGT) Charles D. Butte. It opened our eyes to a part of war that we not only took for granted, but never gave much thought. As Lieutenant Colonel Butte said, "...casualties still occur and our obligation to our fallen comrades remains the same." He said that his unit had training in everything from setting up a cemetery through filling out burial forms, but..."we did not learn how to handle the deceased, armament, ammunition, or to familiarize ourselves with any language which would help us gather information..."

His men handled both friendly and enemy soldiers, as well as civilian casualties. Each was handled with reverence and care. Personal effects were guarded and protected, and if misappropriated would lead to a court martial.

It candidly explained the problems that they had with such little training. He talked of the first deceased soldier that they came in contact with who had been dead for a good while. He was kept from bloating beyond twice the normal size by his uniform and how they learned to deal with it. Mass graves were needed for situations where explosions happened inside of a tank. He felt it important to share, "As gruesome as it may sound, a mess kit cup and spoon were the tools of the trade."

Handling arms and armaments became a routine worry. They were trying to concentrate on the first objective, "...to get the deceased buried...," but it was dangerous to overlook what the soldier might still have in his hand. In one remembered event, there were minor injuries when a soldier they were burying dropped a live grenade that they overlooked in his hands. "As far as I know, no one was ever seriously injured in the field when removing these volatile items..."

They were responsible for training the troops to leave proper identification on their fallen comrades. If the dog tags were missing, they were to leave a note with the body. Civilians were used to dig the graves, but later prisoners of war were used.

Transportation of the bodies was important. "In the summer it was bloating and blood, and in the winter frozen in many shapes...that made the injured in the field job even more of a challenge." They might have to load thirty to three hundred bodies, both friendly and enemy. They would often use two and a half ton trucks to transport the bodies.

On one occasion they were ordered to a town to clean up after the battle, but when they arrived they were warned not to go in because the enemy had recaptured it. They were on a hill overlooking the town when they noticed a couple of bodies in a nearby jeep. When they began loading the bodies, the enemy fired on them, but the shot went long. The second attempt was short, as they were finding the correct range. The soldiers finished up quickly, and as they "kicked it in gear and gunned it... the '88' landed where (they) had been parked."

One story was about the commitment of the men with whom he served. A tank commander, who "lumbered up" in his tank, was asking for help evacuating one of his men from a tank that had taken on enemy fire. "He stated that it was a touching and painful job for him to ask his men to recover the body from the tank due to the condition of the body, plus the fact that the soldier was one of the best thought of men in his unit." It was becoming a "morale problem." As the sergeant was making it clear to the captain whose responsibility it was, a "PFC Wishart stepped up and very boldly and affirmatively said: 'I'll go, Sergeant."

An hour later, PFC Wishart returned with the body on the front of the tank, "acting like a tank commander..." The true tank commander said, "even though they were fired on during the recovery and had to button up at times, it did not deter (him) from doing the job he volunteered to do."

In conclusion to his paper he wrote, "We are proud of our contribution to the war effort. The men of the 603rd worked tirelessly doing the job assigned, and doing it to the best of their ability." He signed it, "Charles D. Butte." His stamp under his name had an American flag, his rank indicated as Lieutenant Colonel, and his address in Riviera Beach, Florida.

Several weeks after reading this report, I received the following information from René :

In the archives of the US Army it is specified

concerning the cemetery of GORRON #1:

PFC Arthur HUDSON:
Time and Date of Burial: *1845-hrs, 21 Aug 44*
Cause of Death: 1   *SW Head, fractured skull.*
Plot: C, Row 1, Grave 10
Date Disinterred: 4 June 1948

PFC Michael KOEPL:
Time and Date of Burial: *1845-hrs, 21 Aug 44*
Cause of Death: *SW Groin.*
Plot: C, Row 1, Grave 6

PFC Jessie PRICE:
Time and Date of Burial: *1830-hrs, 21 Aug 44*
Cause of Death: *SW Groin.*
Plot: C, Row 1, Grave 3
Date Disinterred: 4 June 1948

PVT David WILLIAMS:
Time and Date of Burial: *1830-hrs, 21 Aug 44*
Cause of Death: *SW Chest, fractured skull.*
Plot: C, Row 1, Grave 5
Date Disinterred: 4 June 1948

1st Lt Jason BARRON:
Time and Date of Burial: *1830-hrs, 21 Aug 44*
Cause of Death: *SW Head, Multiple fractures,*
Plot: B, Row 10, Grave 184 *multiple parts missing.*
Date Disinterred: 15 June 1948

S/Sgt Levy Jr. GUIDRY: *1830-hrs, 21 Aug 44*
Time and Date of Burial:
Cause of Death: 2   *Multiple parts fractured,*
Plot: C, Row 1, Grave 7   *multiple parts missing*
Date Disinterred: 4 June 1948
*SW = Shrapnel Wound

Having read Lt. Colonel Butte's report about respectfully collecting the bodies and the importance of documenting as much information about the cause of death as possible, I quickly skimmed this information. I felt little emotion. This was the price of war and I must accept it.

However, that night as I was drifting off to sleep, the description of my uncle's body visited me. I remembered the letter René had written. The letter stated that Arthur LeNoble had found and buried a forearm and a hand. According to the information in the archives, the hand that Arthur LeNoble had found belonged to either Levy Guidry or my uncle. They were the two who were missing body parts. Arthur LeNoble noted that there was a red gold alliance (ring). Levy was not married. Uncle Jason was.

31
The Journey Continues

I had planned to share a few words at the ceremony in Lougé-sur-Maire when the helmet was reclaimed. However, the rain came and I didn't have an opportunity to speak. This is what was in my heart and I would like to share it now.

To our friends in Normandy:

During the early summer of 1944, my uncle, Jason H. Barron, was home in Somerset, Pennsylvania on leave. At 3:00 in the morning, the phone rang and my uncle was ordered to return to duty immediately. His brothers and sisters lined up in the kitchen to kiss him good-bye. As he went out the door, his mother in tears said, "We will never see him again." Unfortunately, this turned out to be true.

I regret that I never got to know my uncle, that he didn't have time to have children of his own, that my father didn't get to share his life with his brother. His widow of 18 months was left to make a new life.We are a very patriotic family. Four brothers of the Barron family served. The journey of this helmet started in WWII. We appreciate the efforts of all of you to honor the soldiers and the loss that their families have suffered.

Thank you to Roger Pillu and Roger Bignon for being the caretaker of this helmet which symbolizes the sacrifice of all soldiers of all nations that gave their lives defending freedom. We thank them for keeping the journey of the helmet alive.

Thank you to René Brideau for making it his mission to research and find the families of the soldiers. And, thank you, René for becoming my email buddy. You have inspired me to search for the other families and to put this book together. It has been my pleasure to get to know the families of David Williams, Levy Guidry, and Jessie C. Price. I will work hard to find the family of Michael Koepl and Arthur Adell Hudson who also died on August 17, 1944, in Lougé-sur-Maire.

I will tell these families of the great honor that has been bestowed upon these six young men. Their families must know that their loved ones have not been forgotten by the devoted people of the area where they gave their lives in pursuit of freedom.

Many Americans are unaware of the care that their loved ones receive. When we visited Brittany Cemetery in St. James, it was very emotional. The superintendent told me that many of the graves are adopted by the French people. I am touched to know that Genevieve Bignon puts flowers on my uncle's grave, just as Roger Pillu's sister, Denise, put flowers on the site of his death many years ago.

The ceremonies of May 23 and May 24, 2009 might seem like a simple gesture. But is a huge act of goodwill between the people of two nations. It fosters understanding. It shows compassion.

In the bell tower in Brittany American Cemetery there is an engraving on the wall. It reads: "as these bells ring,
honored dead rest,
and liberty lives."

Knowing that Jason's life was sacrificed for the liberty of the wonderful people of France gives us comfort.

Merci Beaucoup!

> *Linda Barron Heinrich*
> *May 23, 2009*

Here is our letter to Roger Pillu:

Dear Mr. Pillu,

Words can never express to you our sincere appreciation for what you have done for the Barron Family. You have done a wonderful act of kindness. My father has been very happy since we returned home from France. This experience has provided closure for him.

I have found all the families of the five soldiers that died with my uncle. I have sent to them the testimony that you provided. It has been a great comfort for them to know what happened to their loved ones.

I have thought a lot about you since we

returned home. I didn't get to know much about you. Could you write to us and tell us about yourself - perhaps your work, family, and hobbies.

Again, may I say, many thanks to you. We will never forget our friends in France.

Linda Heinrich

The journey is continuing. I have talked with Kris Bilbrey, David Williams' great- nephew and sent him a package of pictures. I know a day will come when he will travel to Lougé-sur-Maire and experience the pride that I felt.

Frederic, the author of the helmet book, scanned articles from eight different French newspapers into his computer and emailed them to me. They, of course, are in the binder and someday I will have someone read them to me in English. We have come to feel very close to Frederic and Houda and continue to communicate and keep in touch. Frederic sends more information as it becomes available.

I have gone through the hundreds of pictures that we took and added many to my binder where appropriate. I recall the emotions that I felt at each event. Many of them still give me goose bumps.

Stephane Bignon sent us a DVD video that he

had taken. It captures so much that we were unable to put into words when we shared the experience with our friends.

Mayor Gautier sent us a disk of photos taken by Jacques Cabanne which recorded the events for posterity.

Aunt Virginia sent me the American flag that draped Jason's casket, his dog tags, and several documents pertaining to his service in WWII. She wanted me to have them. As I touch them tenderly, I feel a warm connection to my uncle, the man I admire.

After many phone calls, I learned that Eunice died, October 31, 2007, in the state of Oregon. I am very happy to say that she was able to remarry. Dad was very curious about where Jason's Silver Star Medal might be. I obtained the address of Eunice's son and wrote to him to inquire about it. He called me and we talked quite awhile. I informed him about all the events that had taken place. I told him some stories about his mother of which he was unaware.

He said there were boxes packed away in his barn that hadn't been opened after his mother's death. He promised to look through them and see if he could find the Silver Star Medal. He said that if he did find it, he would like for my father to have it.

The reporter from our local newspaper returned and wrote another article about Dad finding closure with the death of his brother. It was picked up by many newspapers across the area, including the Washington Times in Washington, D. C. Dad truly did not find closure, but he received a certain level of peace. Knowing the truth has made him seem years younger since we returned home.

I am completing the process of writing thank you letters to Roger Pillu, Roger and Genevieve Bignon, Mayor Marcel Gautier, Mayor Jean-Marc Allain, Frederic Blais, and René Brideau. How do I tell these people that they have awakened something in me that has changed my life forever?

I was saddened to learn that Arthur LeNoble had died just five months before we went to France to reclaim the helmet. I wish I could have met him.

I have maintained email contact with the families of the five soldiers who died with my uncle on that day. They have become an important part of my life.

I heard that Roger Pillu joined the Bignons and Brideaus when they visited my uncle's grave this year on August 17. Certainly they must have felt a profound closest to Jason on this anniversary.

I have visited my cousins that are a few years older than I am and that I haven't seen in years. I have asked them to share memories. My cousin, Patty showed me a huge box of old pictures. I was amazed to see a picture of Papa Barron when he was a young man....so handsome. I have learn so much about my family history and in so doing, I have learned a lot about myself.

We continue to find information that gives us insight into Uncle Jason's life. I recently found the report of a test that was given to him to determine his fitness to become a commissioned officer. Out of a possible rating of 100, he received only 74 points. I had to chuckle. On the battlefield when duty called, he took charge. He showed his true fitness when he earned the Silver Star. As a teacher, it made me think of how we test students in school. What do the tests we give really tell us about their ability to succeed? There are so many types of intelligence and creativity that we sometimes ignore when evaluating a student's achievement.

We met with the editor of the newspaper in Somerset, Pennsylvania, where Uncle Jason and Dad grew-up. He assigned a reporter, Tiffany Wright, to do a feature article on our experience. When we went to Somerset for the interview, we went to the Court House to see Jason's name on the War Memorial. I was overwhelmed. Without question, this community honors their war heroes. The memorials are well-kept with lovely red, white and blue flowers and benches for meditating.

The Court House itself is beautiful. Dad told us that his father had hauled the large columns from a nearby town with his horse and wagon when it was being built. Dad also showed us the farmhouse where he was born. I realized there was so much that I didn't know.

I have acquired a desire to learn as much as I can about the events of WWII. I watched a documentary of the D-Day invasion, something that previously would not have held my interest. Having visited the towns where the battle occurred, it all made sense to me.

Strangers have sent articles to me concerning true stories of the hardships of WWII. One that was very touching to me was about a man that was a few years older than I am. His father was KIA in Normandy when he was a baby and is buried in France. He never knew where his father had been buried. While vacationing in France, a friend located the grave of the man's father. The following year the friend arranged for him to go to France and visit the cemetery where his father was buried. When he located the marker he said to his father, "So this is where you have been all my life."

Recently, it was my honor to speak with Harry Roach, III. He is the son of the aviator that René 's family rescued. Harry sent information about his father to me. I couldn't put it down. Harry is also writing about the miraculous events that occurred during WWII. The story must be told.

The National Purple Heart Museum in New Windsor, New York, wants to display the story of our six soldiers along with pictures and their purple hearts.

One afternoon I received a telephone call from a lady who lives in a nearby town. She had read the story in the newspaper. She said when she read the part about my uncle being buried in St. James Cemetery it stopped her in her tracks. Her husband had been killed in WWII and he was also buried at St. James. She had never been able to go to his grave. She wanted me to describe the cemetery to her in great detail. Her daughter was only a baby when her father was killed and she was in the process of researching the events that had denied her of a father. I know that by taking on this endeavor she will get to know her father.

As I suspected, friendships continue. Ryan is helping Frederic do research for his next book. Joan speaks with the Bignon family on the phone every other week.

Last week Valerie Bignon sent me an email saying the family plans to visit next year in the U.S. to celebrate Roger and Genevieve's 50th Anniversary. Eight of them will be coming. I became very excited. I had a thought - wouldn't it be great if we could get all the families together for a reunion? Then Valerie sent me another email. They will not be coming to my house. They will be going to Joan's house in New Orleans. At first I was disappointed, but while talking with Joan I learned that she would be able to accommodate all of us. She has a large home on the bay. We can walk to the water and sit on the front porch and rock in the rocking chairs.

That is my kind of vacation. And, she is going to cook for all of us - can you imagine! We extended an invitation to all of the families and everyone is going to make it a priority to attend.

It keeps getting better and better. Who would have thought that a helmet and the gesture of returning it to a soldier's family could have had such a huge impact?

Dad is doing better. I guess we needed to visit the past to fix the present. He has several speaking engagements lined-up and I have been asked to go to several high schools and share our experience.

I received a reply to a letter that I wrote to Roger and Geneviere. It read:

Dear Linda,

We are happy to have received news from you. It was a pleasure to welcome you and your family in our home. These three days were really moving for us, it would not have been the same without your presence.

We think about all this very often. It will stay engraved in our minds. It has been an honour to have you among us, and we all hope to see you very soon.

Send our regards to Emerson. We are happy to know he is feeling well.

On August 17th of August, we put flowers on the place the soldiers were killed, and on the 23rd we went to St. James Cemetery to put flowers on your uncle's grave.

> *Sincerely,*
> *Roger and Geneviere*

There was a post script from their niece:

I translated this letter for my uncle and my aunt. My name is Lucile, I would have liked to attend the ceremony in May but I was studying in England. Writing this letter made me feel as if I took part in this very touching event. I saw the video and all my family, especially my uncle, told me a lot about the three days. They all were very moved. I just want you to know that the young French generation doesn't forget what happened during WWII.

Everyone has an story to share. I found mine in the spring of my 61st year.   As you can see, I am not a word master. I don't know much about the tactical part of World War II. I will leave that to the historians and authors. But, I do know that I have a story to tell. It is a story of a few people in two nations three thousand miles apart, and the helmet that brought them together.

Acknowledgements

Doubts are those little obstacles that get in the way of focusing on your goal. The encouragement of my husband, Brian, and my sons; Brent, Ben, and Nick, helped me overcome those doubts.

I am grateful to Brian for all the research that he did to verify the events that were related in this story. The proof reading skills of Cathy Wallace, Megan Broadwater, Rachael Garlitz, Jan O'Brien Young, Cindy Nalley, Pattie Dell, and Barbara Harrison are very much appreciated.

My gratitude goes to Alex Harrison for sharing his knowledge of publishing and technology. He took an interest in our endeavor to publish this book. He freely and unselfishly gave of his time. He allowed us to call him until three o'clock in the morning.

The information provided by Joan Eymard, Hilton Eymard, Jr., Joan Reilly, Linda Bienvenue, Dale Plaisance, Marjorie Henderson, Inez Nichols, Deborah Miles, Janna White, Norma Ruhling, Linda Smith, Kris Bilbrey, Edward J. Nayes, Carol Meyers, Jeanette Giest, and Scott Paul was invaluable. I must also thank the mystery man who helped me locate Arthur "Adell" Hudson's family.

This story would not have been possible without Roger Pillu, Arthur LeNoble, Roger Bignon, René Brideau,

Frederic Blais, Mayor Marcel Gautier, Mayor Jean-Marc Allain, and the people of Normandy who were dedicated to making this dream come true. A special thanks to Steve Bort and Emmanuel Delaville for the weeks of research that went into identifying the soldiers from F Company that died with my uncle on that fateful day.

My gratitude goes to Genevieve Bignon, Houda Blais, Marie Antoinette Brideau, Gigi Piraud, and the others who supported René and Frederic during their hours of research. Also, my appreciation goes to Joel Marie, Ginette Pitel, Jacques Cabanne, and the others who served on the planning committee. The people of Lougé-sur-Maire and Gorron will always be in our hearts.

Most of all, I thank my father for instilling in our family the love of our great country and an appreciation for the sacrifices that were made so that we know a life of freedom. He never allowed us to forget.

Photo Album
and
Newpaper Article
For more photos and information
visit our website: www.jasonshelmet.com

Our friends, Dave and Debbrah Karstaedt, sit on their 1939
BMW (Bavarian Motor Works) R71 most likely used in the
European Campaign. It could have come to the United States as
ballast in the bottom a ship.
Many were recycled into automobiles.
Dave encouraged me to go to France to get the helmet.

257

Carter Barron adds some levity
to an otherwise solemn occasion.

Many gather at the site of where the soldiers were killed.

Mayor Allain speaks to those who attended the dedication.

Rene and Frederic listen to the speakers
at the Gorron dedication.

259

Somerset native learns of brother's WWII death after 65 years -

THURSDAY, SEPTEMBER 17, 2009 -

By TIFFANY WRIGHT - Daily American Staff Writer

A metal helmet from World War II was the only thing that brought answers about the death of Jason H. Barron to his remaining family members.

It took 65 years for the Barron family to learn how World War II soldier Jason H. Barron died.

Emerson was later convinced to attend the ceremonies along with his daughter and son-in-law, Linda and Brian Heinrich, and other family members. During their three-day trip over Memorial Day, the Barron family received details about Jason.

Jason Barron, a 23-year-old 1st lieutenant in the Army at the time, died on French soil on Aug. 17, 1944, along with the five other men. The soldiers tried to take cover behind a tank, but that would prove to be unsuccessful. Jason died from a piece of shrapnel that ricocheted off nearby trees. The shrapnel entered through one side of Barron's helmet and exited the other. The men were killed 330 yards from a farm house owned by the Bignon family. The area is deemed "Purple Heart Corner" because of the many lives lost there.

Picture-

Emerson Barron holds the battered helmet of his brother, Jason, who was killed in 1944 during World War II in France. The helmet was presented to Barron after he went to France for a ceremony honoring his brother and five other soldiers who died with him.

(Staff photo by Tiffany Wright)

article con'd-

Emerson was about 18 years old and also a member of the military when he heard news of Jason. He was in Mississippi when he received a letter from his father informing him that his older brother had been killed. Four of the Barron sons had served their country.

Linda Heinrich relayed the story that the six soldiers were later found by two men - Roger Pillu and Arthur Lenoble. The men found the helmet with Barron's name and identification number. They stored the historic item *for 60 years, until 2004, when French officials requested World War II items for use in a ceremony recognizing and honoring soldiers of the war.*

During the event Pillu met Roger Bignon, his neighbor during the war. The renewed friendship prompted the men to vow to find the Barron family so they could return Jason's helmet. With the help of friend Rene Brideau and 2 1/2 years of Internet research and Army archives, the family was found.

The search prompted Heinrich to locate family members of the other soldiers. She said she wanted the families to know their relatives were being honored for protecting others' freedom.

"She really started becoming obsessed," Brian Heinrich said of his wife's quest.

Regardless of the other families the Heinrichs and Barrons decided to take part in the ceremonies marking the 65th anniversary.

"I heard about him (Jason) all my life and I wanted to know more about him," Linda Heinrich said.

It took a little more effort to convince her father, who

has never been able to get beyond the death of his brother.

"He wanted to go, but it's hard to go where the pain is," she said.

The event was more extravagant than expected.

"We finally realized why they wanted us there," Heinrich said. "It ended up being a huge ceremony and they really treated daddy like royalty."

A plaque was presented honoring the men. The Bignon family invited the families to stay on the farm.

"This right here," Brian said pointing to the battered helmet, "was the reason for all of this happening."

Emerson is still overwhelmed with emotions talking about his brother.

"From the time it happened I've had recurring dreams of my brother coming home," he said as he choked up and his eyes welled with tears. "He gets out of his car and walks past me, but never talks to me."

The Barron family never knew how or where their son

and brother was killed. While finding out what happened may have brought peace to some, it still has not set in for Emerson.

"I thought it was going to bring me closure, but that hasn't happened yet," he said.

He still is grateful for the hospitality the French showed the families of the soldiers.

"I told them that I would be the best ambassador for France," he said.

Brian Heinrich said most Americans have the impression that the French do not appreciate what U.S. soldiers did for them.

"We realize now that's not the case," he said.

"Especially in Normandy, the people are so grateful for their liberation from the Germans."

Linda Heinrich said while many of the conversations were lost in translation, one message was certain.

"The language is difficult to understand, but the language of the heart is loud and clear," she said.

Jason Barron was married to a woman named Eunice for only 18 months. After he died he was awarded the Silver Star, the third-highest military honor, as well as the Purple Heart. Of the six soldiers, Jason Barron is the only one whose body was not returned to the U.S. for burial, but Emerson said he is OK with that.

"It's fine. Let him stay over there," he said.

Barron's remains are at Brittany American Cemetery and Memorial in St. James, France. He is among more than 4,000 others. Linda Heinrich said the cemetery seems similar to that of Arlington National Cemetery in Virginia.

The Heinrichs are writing a book called "Jason's Helmet" that is due for publication this fall. They want people to know the sacrifice soldiers made during war as well as how Memorial Day now means something more to them.

(Tiffany Wright may be contacted at tiffanyw@dailyamerican.com.
Comment on the online story at dailyamerican.com.)

Used with permission in this book.

Challenge to the Reader

If reading our story has aroused an interest in you to learn about a family member or friend who was served in World War II, I would encourage you to do the research. It is very rewarding and an honor to those who gave their lives for our freedom.

If your loved one served in the European Theater, it is even more rewarding to take a trip to Normandy and see for yourselves.

This book would also lend itself to school research projects. By selecting a soldier and learning more about his or her service, students could better understand how lives are affected by war. There are many websites available to use during research.

Bibliography

Website that I have found to be of value:

www.3ad.com, Spearhead in the West
www.thepurpleheart.com
www.ancestery.com
www.archives.com
www.c3airsoft.com
www.hearld-mail.com
www.dailyamerican.com
www.world-war-2-planes.com
www.demons7th.com

We would like to recommend to you the book that inspired me to continue my research:

Helmets of the ETO: A Historical and Technical Guide
By Regis Giard and Frederic Blais
Available on www.amazon.com

Brian is a retired Physical Education teacher. He enjoys his family first, and concurs that morning coffee on the back deck has top priority. His faith and children, Brent, Ben and Nick have kept him centered. Brian is a performer at heart in a variety of venues. He enjoys writing songs and, in his spare time, he is developing the skills to be a handyman around the house. It was an honor to accompany his wife, Linda, and father-in-law, Emerson, to retrieve Jason's helmet and to assist Linda in sharing her story.

Recently, Linda retired from Washington County Public Schools as a Staff Development Specialist. Since her retirement, Linda is enjoying spending time with her family, traveling, hiking, volunteering, writing, and having morning coffee with her husband. She and Brian live in Hagerstown, Maryland. Her sons, Brent, Benjamin, and Nicholas, have been her greatest supporters. Her plans for the future include reminding young people that they have a very precious gift - freedom.